a tree across my road

Other books by Larry Yeagley:
How to Get Beyond Loneliness
Life After Loss
Touched by Fire

To order, call 1-800-765-6955.
Visit us at www.reviewandherald.com for information on other
Review and Herald® products.

a tree across my road

Larry Yeagley

REVIEW AND HERALD® PUBLISHING ASSOCIATION
HAGERSTOWN, MD 21740

The author assumes full responsibility for the accuracy of all facts and quotations as cited in this book.

Texts credited to Message are from *The Message.* Copyright © 1993, 1994, 1995, 1996. Used by permission of NavPress Publishing Group.
Scripture quotations marked NASB are from the *New American Standard Bible,* © The Lockman Foundation 1960, 1962, 1963, 1968, 1971, 1972, 1973, 1975, 1977.
Texts credited to NIV are from the *Holy Bible, New International Version.* Copyright © 1973, 1978, 1984, International Bible Society. Used by permission of Zondervan Bible Publishers.
Bible texts credited to NRSV are from the New Revised Standard Version of the Bible, copyright © 1989 by the Division of Christian Education of the National Council of the Churches of Christ in the U.S.A. Used by permission.

This book was
Edited by Tompaul Wheeler
Cover design by Leumas Design
Cover photo by Getty Images
Interior design by Candy Harvey
Eletronic makeup by Shirley M. Bolivar
Typeset: 12/15 Bembo

PRINTED IN U.S.A.

10 09 08 07 06   5 4 3 2 1

R&H Cataloging Service
Yeagley, Lawrence Robert, 1933-   .
    A tree across my road.

    1. Religious life.   2. Spiritual life.   I. Title

                    248

ISBN 978-0-8280-1891-3

*To the hundreds of courageous people
who have attended bereavement support groups
that I have conducted during the last 30 years.*

*They have confronted their fallen trees
and moved beyond by the rich grace of God.*

Contents

Preface

A friend of mine told me he doesn't enjoy books that he must read through in order to understand the topic. He'd rather catch a short message that he can plant in his mind like a seed to grow throughout the day.

I wrote these short essays to be seeds that can be used in personal devotions or as discussion starters in small groups. I hope to draw your attention to little events in life that are not just happenstance, but lessons to draw you closer to God and to others.

CHAPTER 1

Facing Difficulties

A TREE ACROSS MY ROAD

"You're bound to earn a scholarship if you determine to never miss a house," promised the sales trainer. NEVER MISS A HOUSE became my mantra as I sold religious books in the hills and hollows of Adams County, Ohio. My rusty 1940 Studebaker took me over rough terrain to accomplish my goal.

I heard about a small settlement tucked between two ridges, but I didn't know how to get there. One day I took a narrow dirt road to visit an elderly couple living in a log cabin. I asked them how to get to the settlement. "Keep a-goin' up this road. At the top of the ridge you'll see the settlement in the holler," they assured me.

Slowly I chugged my way around rocks and mud puddles. At times I feared crushing the under parts of the old "Studie." As I neared the top of the ridge two medium-sized trees lay across the road. For the next half hour I tugged at those trees until my "blue wonder" was able to scrape through.

The trees across my road were only the first roadblock. The few families in the hollow were conditioned by the preacher to resist all salesmen, especially religious book salesmen. I met the preacher in his tobacco field where he chewed his own tobacco and preached me a sermon about needing nothing but the Word.

The preacher's two daughters descended on us like vultures. One leaned on my sales companion's shoulder as he showed his book to the resistant preacher's wife. The other climbed into the front seat of the "Studie" and squeezed tight against me as she begged for a ride. My visit to the hollow was totally surprising, hilarious, and unprofitable.

On my weekly trip from Portsmouth, Ohio, to Ironton, Ohio, the traffic came to a complete standstill. Word passed from one motorist to another that the underpass was flooded after the torrential rainfall. I'd be late to my appointment if I returned to Portsmouth, crossed the Ohio River, and crossed into Ohio at Ashland, Kentucky. I asked a motorist if there was a closer way to Ironton. "Yep, you can fly," he quipped.

I made a U turn and drove in to a farmer's barnyard. The farmer met me at the gate. "Tell me, friend," I called, "how can I get to Ironton other than going by way of Route 52?"

"Well," he mused, "if you don't mind gettin' that pretty powder blue Ford a little muddy, I can get you there. See that corn field yonder? If you gun that Ford real good, go through the barnyard and through the cornfield, you'll come to a gravel road. Don't let up on the gas. Get stuck in that mud, and you'll never get out. Turn right on the gravel, and it'll take you right into Ironton."

Mud flew off the tires and spattered my windshield, but I reached the gravel road. Two miles from the town line a huge oak tree lay across the road. I feared I'd never get to town.

I noticed a small house just before I came upon the fallen tree. I went back to that house and asked the lady how I could get to Ironton. She directed me down another gravel road. Eight miles later I pulled my blue Falcon up to the church just in time for my appointment.

While visiting my son in Gentry, Arkansas, a tornado ripped through and felled a huge oak, completely blocking his driveway. At six in the morning in pouring rain we chainsawed and tugged until we cleared the tree from the driveway. A half mile later three sheriffs stopped us while men removed another tree from the highway. We discovered that a neighbor had lost power due to fallen trees and his driveway was blocked by trees. By the time we dealt with fallen trees, my son was late for work.

I don't know if you have ever had a tree across your road. I do know that most of us have had well-devised plans interrupted and glorious goals shattered by situations beyond our control. It's like a tree across the road when we are in a hurry to go somewhere—frustrating, worrisome, hope-shattering, and often faith-shattering. We can lose sight of the open road beyond the fallen tree, because the tree is the only thing we can see.

Some fallen trees are ultimately viewed as providential interventions. Others are perceived as hurdles that we will never be able to surmount. Some fallen trees puzzle us the rest of our days. At times fallen trees leave gaping holes that take years to restore. We might even consider a fallen tree a way of opening and broadening our view.

No matter how we eventually look at a tree across our road, the fallen tree stops us in our tracks. We have to size up the situation, examine our options, and determine how we can resume our journey.

My friend Carl invited me to dinner the day after a severe wind storm in Texas. While his wife put the finishing touches to the meal, Carl took me out to see his large garden. Three large plum trees bordered the garden. Hundreds of green, unripe plums were strewn across the ground. "Carl," I said, "what a pity to lose all these plums. You must be sick about this."

"The Lord is good, Larry," Carl responded. "Just think about it. Now that these unripe plums have blown off the trees, the ones that remain will get more energy from the tree and become larger and sweeter."

I thought about the words of a teacher who tried to console me about a difficult situation. "There are times when what we have lost is less important than what we do with what we have left." Carl seemed to operate on that principle.

Therese A. Rando, grief therapist, talks about the assumptive world each of us creates. We assume that life will bring a good education, a well-paying career, a loving spouse, two obedient children, and a spacious home in the country. Unfortunately, our assumptive world and reality sometimes clash.

My son has written dramas for summer camps for many years. When he began designing camp fire programs, he asked me to write one of the dramas.

At the end of the camping season I visited the camp to watch the camp staff act out my drama. The actors and actresses adapted their lines to their own liking so that what I envisioned in the writing was very different from the production. I realized that I had not visualized camp children as I wrote the script. The camp staff knew their children and injected humor and expressions that would hold their attention.

You may have written and rewritten your life script over the years, only to find that your actual life production only slightly resembles the script. I saw a demonstration of that at my wife's fiftieth high school reunion. Twenty-five of her classmates sat around a circle and shared the events of life since high school graduation. An aspiring minister became a doctor. One fellow who vowed never to become a minister did so after years of teaching. Several who were wildly in love in high school were into their second or third marriage.

I've met a few people who have had their assumptive world shattered, yet insisted on living in their assumptive world. A classmate of mine had a serious speech impediment. He was studying for the ministry against his advisor's counsel. Many years later I learned that he was still applying for a church position. He will probably spend the rest of his life seeking a pulpit assignment.

Given a chain saw, fallen trees can be cleared from our roadways, but the situational trees in our lives can be insurmountable. The stories about people who climb mountains after losing limbs are inspiring, but the philosophy that you can do whatever you set your heart on has flaws. Sometimes changing your route is the better part of wisdom.

The apostle Paul had some trees across his road that were placed there by God. The Scripture says that he intended to preach in some towns, but the Spirit told him not to go. God also directed him to different destinations, yet arriving at those destinations sometimes brought difficulty to him. Paul dreamt that a man from Macedonia told him to come there, only to find himself in jail. The outcome was the conversion of the jailer and his family.

We live in a world where trees fall across our road. There's a lot of rhetoric about who drops the trees. I consider this conjecture a waste of time. I'd rather ask God for wisdom to decide how to deal with the fallen trees. I believe He gives us wisdom to do just that. He also has the power to help us live for Him, whether it be on the same road or on a different path.

NEGATIVES TO POSITIVES

During World War II my brother loved to have furloughs from the Coast Guard so he could come home on the train. Many servicemen didn't have that luxury. They hitchhiked. Some cities provided shelters next to the highway so they could be out of the weather while waiting for a ride. My parents enjoyed giving a military man a lift.

For years after the war motorists were willing to pick up hitch-hikers. It was relatively safe, but the danger and uncertainty increased as years passed.

I attended school in Philadelphia and Washington, D.C., in the late 1940s and early 1950s. Due to limited finances I used this method of transportation to go home on weekends. A number of trips convinced me that God protected me and used me to touch people in need.

My mother had surgery in a Lancaster, Pennsylvania, hospital. I walked a mile to a main road near Washington and stuck out my thumb. A friendly couple took me to the center of Baltimore and dropped me off. I walked for an hour to reach the highway to York. Within 10 minutes a man picked me up and took me all the way to Lancaster. After a 30-minute walk to the hospital I learned that my mother had been discharged about the time I arrived in the city.

Determined to see my mother, I walked to the highway to Lebanon where I waited an hour before a young man in an old car screeched to a stop. I jumped into the front seat and instantly heard the voice of H.M.S. Richards, Sr., of the *Voice of Prophecy* radio program. We rode along in silence listening to Richards talking about how God's power changes lives. When the program ended, he turned off the radio, and we talked about his spiritual struggles.

After an hour he said, "My home was back there about 15 miles. Why don't I take you to your house, then I'll turn around and go home." I invited him in to meet my parents and fixed both of us a meal. I gave him some religious books from my mother's library, and he left feeling encouraged.

As I waited for a ride in Lancaster, I questioned why I had missed seeing my mother in the hospital and why so many motorists passed by without stopping. As I bid my new friend farewell, I no longer questioned. God had a plan.

God can use seeming negatives to open doors for people who

need what we can provide. I learned this again in Manchester, Ohio, where I sold religious books in the summer of 1952.

On Saturday nights the local folk living in the hills and hollows came to town to socialize. Old men sat on benches and curbs eating popcorn and smoking their homegrown tobacco. Women shopped in the few stores open late. Young people walked the sidewalks or went to the only theater in town. Guys with cars cruised the only main street. Parking was on the diagonal and mighty scarce on Saturday night.

Being new in town, I decided to park, roam the street, and talk to people who just might be future customers. Just as I slowed down to enter a parking space, a young man came through the traffic light on yellow and struck the back end of my car. My car was not damaged, but he broke his grill and one headlight.

Neither of us had insurance, so I agreed to help with his repairs even though I was not at fault. The local constable came upon the scene and was satisfied that we had settled in a friendly fashion. He wrote no citations. Two days later the young man stopped by the cottage where I was staying and told me that he found a grill and a headlight in the junkyard and was going to fix it himself.

A week later I noticed someone cultivating a tobacco patch with a mule. I walked out to the field to sell a book. To my surprise it was the young man who had struck my car. He asked me to visit his parents up on the ridge. Their house had burned down the night we had the collision. They were living in a chicken house with no beds, tables, or chairs.

Their living conditions wounded my heart. I contacted the members of the little Manchester Seventh-day Adventist Church. Within days they supplied their needs. I'm still puzzled about how that small congregation did so much. An accident drew two young men together and opened a door to help a destitute family.

I often think of the One who had no permanent place to lay his head. Jesus left the majesty of heaven and was born into a simple home. The wealth of the world was the product of His hand, but He lived from hand to mouth. Did His situation hinder Him?

Passing through a village, Jesus healed scores of sick people. Outcasts were restored to their communities. Hopeless people received hope. Jesus turned His negatives into positives.

If only I could always remember that God is already working to turn my negatives into positives. God has a handle on things before I begin to deal with my negatives. Why do I try to do it by myself?

Abraham took his son to the mountain, built an altar, placed the fuel on top, and began to sacrifice his boy Isaac. How he managed to explain it to his son without Isaac heading down the mountain, I'm not sure. The knife was poised, but God stopped Abraham's arm in midair. He saw a lamb struggling in a thorny bush behind him. His son was spared by the substitute.

Abraham was so grateful that he called that place Jehovah-jireh. One Hebrew scholar gave me his translation of the word: "The God who sees ahead, provides ahead."

That's what God does with my negatives.

FALLING, FAILING, OR SOARING?

Falling can result in injury or even death. Dreams of falling can awaken you in a sweat. Crossing a gushing stream on a log while walking upright can soon reduce you to a seated position with both legs straddling the log.

I once convinced my wife to climb the Bee Hive at Bar Harbor, Maine. Near the top we had to climb straight up using hand holds driven into the granite. That was followed by walking on a narrow grating from which we could see tree tops far below. A mere mention of that climb causes her to say, "I've never forgiven you for taking me on that excursion."

In spite of the fear of falling, some people get a thrill from it. One of my barbers broke both legs while sky diving, but he jumped again after his legs healed. One of my sons bungee jumped off a high tower. A friend of mine joined his buddies in jumping from a tree limb 40 feet from the surface of the water in a stone quarry. The water was 80 feet deep. In Orlando I watched youth being strapped into the cart of the Sling Shot. Using pneumatic technology, the Sling Shot caused them to experience 2.5g's as they catapulted far above 222 feet support towers. The cart rolled upside down as they plunged toward earth. They paid $25 each for the privilege.

In Texas my sons and their friends coaxed me to climb a high tower and descend a waterslide that was almost perpendicular to the ground. Sitting at the top, I could not see the slide in front of me. The attendant raised the bar and told me to push off. Fear gripped me, but I pushed off. I barely felt the surface of the slide. In seconds my body plunged into the pool below. A digital device clocked my speed at 39 miles per hour. Just writing about it makes me feel the fear.

The fear of failing when attempting a new activity can be just as foreboding as the thought of hang-gliding off a cliff. My first attempt at selling religious books was just such a heart-pounding event. A polite lady listened to my sales pitch and smiled as she saw the sweat running down my face and my hands shaking as I turned the pages of my prospectus. She bought a book out of sheer pity.

Going to a job interview can bring fear of falling flat on your face. Taking a crucial exam when applying for medical school can unnerve you. Appearing before a superior in the armed forces because of an infraction can make you tremble inside. It is human to fear falling and failing.

We're in good company when we fear. God asked Jeremiah to give an unpopular message to the people of Judah. Jeremiah protested, "O Lord, I can't do that. I don't know how to speak. I'm just a youth." God said, "Jeremiah, I appointed you to be a prophet before you were born. Don't be afraid of the people. Don't say you're just a youth. Go. Everywhere I send you, I will be with you and put words in your mouth."

We don't see a lot of true prophets running around today, but God still puts words in the mouths of ordinary people who fear falling and failing.

Isaiah wrote that those who wait for the Lord will become stronger and soar like eagles. In that case we don't need to be afraid of falling or failing. When God gives you wings you ride the thermals of difficulty.

Have you ever ridden in a glider? My sons each went up near Elmira, New York. A towplane pulled them up to 5,000 feet and cut them loose. The pilot went in search of thermals. When he found one, he circled higher and higher, riding the rising warm air.

Riding on the wings of God's power, we can overcome the forces of evil. The devil must become furious when his destructive forces merely elevate the person who waits on the Lord.

In the 26 years I've served as hospice chaplain I have seen people rise above life-threatening illness. Instead of depressing them, the diagnosis lifted them closer to God. They were unafraid of falling asleep in death because underneath were the everlasting arms. Of course, there were dark times, but the prevailing direction was upward. They knew that resurrection day would seem only a moment after death, when they'd soar upward in an angel cloud, unafraid of falling through space.

Someday I'm going to take a glider ride simply to experience the feeling of silently and effortlessly rising above our troubled world.

TAKE UP YOUR CROSS

I saw a middle-aged man carrying a wooden cross along Route

412 in Siloam Springs, Arkansas. There wasn't anything unusual about him. He wore a pair of denims and a clean, long-sleeved shirt, a comfortable pair of walking shoes on his feet. The unusual part of the whole scene was the wheel on the end of his cross. I suppose it made carrying the fairly lightweight cross a little easier.

Jesus asked us to take up our cross and follow Him. Could He have meant an actual wooden cross? Or was He referring to a set of circumstances that require courage to live for Him?

Hilda took her three daughters to church every week. Every week her husband berated her. He thought church was an unnecessary interruption of household duties. As she left for church she called a cheerful goodbye and swallowed the tears. No wheels on that cross.

Edward was afflicted with throat cancer. He could not speak and had to be fed by a tube. He lost his 18-year-old son to an accident. He and his wife lived in a small trailer house surrounded by a fence that kept out the neighbor's vicious dogs. They had no family nearby, but they rejoiced to have each other. The highlight of Edward's day was to hear his wife read the Bible each morning and each evening. His doctor told him to enjoy life as much as possible, because it was only a matter of time. His was a heavy cross, but there was no wheel attached.

Ann's husband told her that the day she joined the church, he would walk out and never return. Some people told Ann that her marriage was more important than church, but she knew that Jesus must take first place in her life. She returned home to an empty house. How about that for a cross?

As I travel across America I frequently see three wooden crosses standing along the road. The center cross is yellow, and the others are white. In Missouri I saw a cross that appeared to be 10 stories high. Churches have crosses attached to their buildings. Some churches are built in the shape of a cross. But no matter how high or expensive, building a cross is simple in contrast to carrying one.

Occasionally I flip through the TV channels and come upon a musical group holding microphones close to their mouths and crooning about the cross. They close their eyes and raise their hands at what seem to me inappropriate places in the lyrics. It's easy to sing about the cross. Try carrying one.

I sometimes watch a TV preacher in Florida preaching about taking up the cross. His church has multiple spires that rise high above the ground. The interior of the church is decorated with the very best material. He stands in a pulpit high above the congregation dressed in an ornate robe. Talking about the cross is easy. Try living the kingdom life when you are the only person in your family who shares your convictions. No wheels on that cross!

The apostle had a cross—a physical malady. He prayed to get rid of it, but God conveyed to him in some way that His grace was sufficient. Paul could live with his cross because he knew that he was a sojourner in a strange land traveling to a land where crosses would not exist.

That cross-carrying fellow on 412 made an impact on me. Aside from being curious about his agenda, I asked myself if I would have the courage to carry a wooden cross with a wheel. Would I fear making a spectacle of myself?

Is my faith in God strong enough to live my convictions when I am the only person holding them? Do I really believe that the one who died on a cross will give me the strength to face opposition, even from family and close friends?

JUST SING A SONG

If you should happen to be in Mountain Home, Arkansas, in the evening, you'll have a real mountain treat. By the time the sun sets musicians leave their homes in the hills and hollows and gather in groups around the village square. Fiddles, jaw harps, guitars, banjos, harmonicas, and dulcimers can be seen in abundance. Someone calls out the title of a country song. Another calls out the key signature. The song continues until all the instruments have had a chance to take the lead. If you can sing, they'll be happy to accompany you. When the music is lively, some folks will dance. None of the players and singers are professional. They come not to impress, but to have a good time.

I took my family to a Christmas Eve worship service in National Cathedral in Washington, D.C. We arrived a half hour before the doors opened. The bitter cold wind prompted total strangers to huddle close to each other for protection. A clear voice began singing "Silent Night." In moments the entire crowd was singing the carol. We forgot the cold as one carol after another lifted our spirits.

The Amish youth in my neighborhood gather every other Sunday evening for a "sing" preceded by a delicious meal. Some songs are sung in German, some in English. The guys and girls make eye contact as they sing, followed by blushing and broad smiles. Promptly at 8:00 they sing "Blessed Be the Tie That Binds," then head for their buggies to escort their special friend home the long way.

In Port au Prince, Haiti, I joined dozens of high school students on a walk up a mountain. Near the top we entered a cave lighted by candles. After reading the Bible the students began to sing. Their voices echoed off the hard surfaces of the cave, prompting them to sing sweetly with four-part harmony.

Something spiritual happens when God's children sing. When our oldest son was four, he was admitted to the hospital the evening before his tonsillectomy. When we returned an hour before the surgery, the head nurse sighed, "Am I ever glad to see you! Jeff sang 'Jesus Loves Me' far into the night, keeping the other patients awake."

Singing may have kept other children awake, but it also kept Jeff's mind off his upcoming encounter with the surgeon.

Paul and Silas of New Testament fame were thrown into jail for preaching the Good News. Instead of complaining, they sang and prayed. Their songs transformed their fellow prisoners. Don't you wish you could have heard their courageous voices?

African slaves in America were imprisoned by wealthy plantation owners. Many of them were treated cruelly. Family members were separated, causing deep loneliness. In the drudgery of cotton fields under scorching southern sun they sang about when their troubles would be over. Their singing transported their minds to the heavenly land where slavery would be gone.

The book of Revelation pictures redeemed people from all walks of life and all ethnic backgrounds worshiping God by singing around the throne of God. No barriers. One theme—deliverance from the dungeon of this sin-cursed world.

Music was meant to draw people together. It was meant to bring joy and peace, not rancor, accusing words, and division. That's what music can do for us today and throughout eternity

Karen Carpenter used to sing a song, "Don't worry that it's not good enough for anyone else to hear, just sing, sing a song."

That's what a single mother was doing as she performed a menial task. I heard the music and followed the sound until I saw her bent over her work, singing "Amazing Grace" with deep feeling. I told her how much her song encouraged me. She smiled and said, "Thank God."

I'm sure her song reached the ears of God. Your song touches His heart also. So, just sing. Sing from your heart!

CHAPTER 2

God's Eternal Love

PROUD FATHERS

Jacob looked into the eyes of his newborn son. "You're a big fellow. It won't be long until you're working in the stable and fields with me." His words burst with first-time-father pride.

Weeks after Benny's birth I walked into the cow stable at milking time. Hanging from a rafter hook was a baby swing holding Benny, swinging and watching his Amish mother and father milking the large Jersey herd.

When Benny was a year old, I walked past the hayfield where Jacob was fluffing the drying hay with his side delivery rake pulled by two large Belgians. When Jacob pulled over to the edge of the road to chat, I noticed Benny seated in a car seat fastened to a homemade platform on the rake. His little dark eyes were taking in every move of the horses. When I returned from my walk, Jacob stopped the team and held Benny high in the air to wave to me. Jacob's pride was unmistakable.

A Tree Across My Road

Robert is my 5-year-old Amish friend. He loves to play ball with me and loves even more to blow my car horn. He calls it horn tootin'. When I pull my Ford into the driveway of his home his eyes sparkle and his freckled face bursts into a smile that covers his whole face.

One day I went to visit his father, David, on business. As I looked toward the back pasture I saw a bicycle coming down the path behind the cows. David was peddling and Robert was riding in a seat behind his father. Both had smiles worth a million dollars.

A week later I stopped by the farm and found David repairing the tongue on his manure spreader. Robert was lying in the grass watching his father's every move. "Are you helping your Daddy?" I asked. "Yah," was his quick reply. I quickly looked at David and caught that proud-to-be-his-Daddy smile.

Nostalgia sweeps over me when I watch Amish fathers and their children. I loved to be with my father as a boy My chest swelled when he told people I was a good boy. I walked miles behind the plow and cultivator just to be near my father. As a teenager I'd stand on the drawbar of his F-20 Farmall tractor. The front wheels would sometimes leave the ground as my father plowed up the hill. Instantly he would tramp on the left or right wheel brake and the front end would drop. He'd look back at me with that "oops" expression on his face and say, "Watch the way I do this. You'll be doing it on your own some day."

Years later my father visited me in Ohio where I was pastoring a church. I took him on pastoral visits and proudly introduced him to my parishioners. They would say complimentary things about me, and my father instantly agreed. What a boost to my ego!

Can you imagine Adam and Eve strolling with God in the Garden of Eden in the cool of the day? God says, "You are special to Me. I formed you out of clay and breathed life into you. You're exactly what I had in mind. You are My treasure."

In contrast, can you imagine how they felt as they were hiding from God? They must have feared the worst, but to their surprise, God told them there was hope. He outlined His plan to restore them to His image. Some readers of the book of Genesis see only a punitive God, but I see the Creator with tears running down His face as He asks, "Where are you?"

In spite of their rebellion, God proudly came close to them as a father draws his child close to his chest. And when the drama of the great controversy is all over, God will exult over His redeemed family. He will triumphantly lead us to the heavenly home He has prepared for us. I have a hunch that we will spend eternity amazed at His love that insisted on a close parent-child relationship in spite of our waywardness.

MISTAKEN IDENTITY

As I walked toward the pier at Bar Harbor, Maine, an elderly man I did not recognize approached me from the end of the pier. As he came near, his body language told me that he recognized me. He became excited as he said, "Well, Fred, I haven't seen you in ages. How are you doing, my friend?"

I responded, "I'm doing just fine. And how have you been?"

He told me a bit about his recent life, but as he did so, a bewildered look crossed his face. He said, "Oh, I'm sorry! I thought you were Fred Adams. You favor him a lot."

I tried to ease his embarrassment. "That's just fine! I'm happy to make a new friend."

We introduced ourselves and shared a few facts about our background. We both laughed at the mistaken identity and parted ways.

A friend attended a church homecoming. She had not been there in years. She enthusiastically sat next to a woman and called her by the wrong name. The woman smiled, knowing that time can erase names and faces and can even mix them well.

Sometimes mistaken identity can be complimentary. When you call a mother by her daughter's name, she looks in the mirror to see if she has really reversed the aging process.

In the book of Isaiah the prophet declares that God knows us by name. The Gospels state that the hairs of our head are all numbered. I'm not sure that the last statement can be taken literally, but it does mean that God knows us better than we know ourselves. He can never be accused of mistaken identity.

I don't understand how God does it, but on second thought, I have known people who have an uncanny ability to remember names.

A health educator and I conducted a week of spiritual and health emphasis at an elementary school. She went from classroom to classroom asking each child his or her name. The next day and all week she called each child by name. Months later she met a man in the hospital. Upon learning his name she said, "Oh, you must be Danny's father. I met him at school."

If a few mortals can remember names, why not God?

When someone calls us by the wrong name, we sometimes jokingly say, "That's OK. Just so you don't call me late for dinner." We may pass it off lightly, but we do feel good when we are remembered accurately.

When God remembers us by name, it tells us that we are special to Him. It is more than a memory technique. He is truly interested in every aspect of our life. The psalmist declared that God knows our lying down and our rising up. He knows our heart's desires. He understands everything behind our name.

DID YOU FORGET?

Yes, you have! You've gone to the basement for a jar of peaches, stood in the middle of the floor, and said to yourself, "Now, what did I come down here to get?"

Admit it! You've climbed into your van and started your trip to visit a good friend, but had to stop at the end of the driveway to ask yourself, "Let's see, how do I get there?"

I was perturbed at my lapses of memory when I heard Robert Serkin performing a long Mozart piano concerto with the Lansing Symphony Orchestra. He played the whole composition without a single note in front of him. He never looked worried about making his entries. In fact, he anticipated them with a smile on his face.

A man arrived on my college campus in the evening and was given a copy of the most recent *Time* magazine. The next morning as the students arrived at assembly, they were given copies of the same issue of *Time*. They asked questions about ads and articles on specific pages. The man described the items in detail.

Our son, newly licensed to drive, went to New York City with the New England Youth Ensemble. The director asked him to drive the station wagon that pulled the trailer full of instruments back to Clinton, Massachusetts. It was night and the three passengers were sleeping. I asked him how he managed to thread his way through the tangle of parkways and turnpikes. "Nothing to it," was his reply. "I looked at the map and memorized my route." I sure can't relate—I depend on my wife to call out the turns as we take a trip.

Have you ever been amazed at a person who calls you by name after meeting you for the first time a year before? I have. Then I struggled to remember their name, going through all the letters of the alphabet in an attempt to retrieve the name from my mental file cabinet.

I have often wished for the chance to buy more memory like I do for my desktop computer.

When I read the Bible I notice that God asked people to *remember* the deliverance from Egyptian bondage by celebrating the Passover. He said to *remember* the Sabbath to keep it holy. He asked parents to speak the laws of the Lord to their children every morning. Jesus went into the synagogue every Sabbath and either read or listened to the prophets and the psalms. Memory is important to God.

Memory specialists claim that we remember people, places, and events that are highly valued and enjoyed. They also apply the old adage "use it or lose it."

One thing I know for sure: God never forgets me. A mother may forget her child, but God never has a memory lapse when it comes to who I am, and what is important to my eternal well-being.

IN THE MIDDLE OF IT ALL

The preaching of H.M.S. Richards, Sr., the longtime speaker of the *Voice of Prophecy* radio broadcast, has enthralled me from boyhood. When he came to our local camp meeting, I sat on the front row of seats, listening to every word. He told a story that I have tried to find in a book, but never have. I'll share it with you in hopes that it will stay with you as long as I have loved it.

A minister and his 8-year-old daughter were returning to their home in Europe aboard a steamship. They had just lost wife and mother to death in America. They were planning to bury her in the homeland.

One evening they were walking on the deck of the ship. The sky was clear, and the air was warm. The daughter had heard her father preaching about God's love many times. Now in a reflective mood, she asked, "Daddy, is God's love as deep as this ocean?"

"Yes, it is," he assured her.

"Is God's love as wide as this ocean?" she continued.

"Of course it is," he told her.

"Is God's love as high as the sky?" she asked.

"Oh, it certainly is, dear," he agreed.

"Well then, Daddy," the daughter concluded, "we must be in the middle of it all!"

The little girl would have liked what the apostle Paul wrote in Romans 8. "So, what do you think? . . . If God didn't hesitate to put everything on the line for us, embracing our condition and exposing himself to the worst by sending his own Son, is there anything else he wouldn't gladly and freely do for us? And who would dare tangle with God by messing with one of God's chosen? Who would dare even to point a finger? The One who died for us—who was raised to life for us!—is in the presence of God at this very moment sticking up for us. Do you think anyone is going to be able to drive a wedge between us and Christ's love for us? There is no way!" (Message). The same passage in another version says, "For I am convinced that neither death nor life, neither angels nor demons, neither the present nor the future, nor any powers, neither height nor depth, nor anything else in all creation, will be able to separate us from the love of God that is in Christ Jesus our Lord" (Rom. 8:38, 39, NIV).

Everyone has a need to be loved unconditionally. Everyone needs to have the assurance that love never fails.

Henri J. M. Nouwen spoke about followers of God being living reminders of Jesus. Just as Jesus was a demonstration of God's unconditional love, so we can be a demonstration of God's unconditional love.

When we are truly present to a person in need, God's love is all around that person. We are in the middle of it all. How awesome to be the conveyor of such love!

CHAPTER 3

Life Is for Living

LOOKING FORWARD

My 9-year-old grandson telephoned to say, "Guess what! I'm now using underarm deodorant!"

He visited his third-grade room at the end of his second grade. In an effort to preserve the pleasant aroma in her classroom, the teacher highly recommended the use of deodorant, especially to the active boys. My grandson was not offended. To him it was a rite of passage.

What a contrast to the older generation who love to go to church and sing, "Never grow old, never grow old, in the land where we'll never grow old."

I remember sneaking into my father's shaving kit and whacking off the peach fuzz on my upper lip. I was 14. For days I ran my fingers upward across my upper lip to feel that bristly effect. I was elated to have arrived at manhood.

Now I rue the day I began shaving. At times I threaten to grow a beard, much to my wife's groans.

Remember your first solo trip behind the wheel of your parents' car or your own junker? Mine was a 1940 Studebaker. Half of the doors had rusted away, but sheet metal kept the rain from entering. The floorboards were rusted out. Plywood kept my feet from hitting the ground. The car dealer installed a rebuilt engine, but never thought to check the condition of the radiator that needed a rebore job. When I climbed a hill, I had to stop until the engine cooled. On a trip to Ohio I had two flat tires, and the dimmer switch got stuck on high beam. Despite the flaws, I felt like a rich man behind the wheel of that blue wonder. I loved cruising through town.

Now try to contrast that first-car day to the possibility of walking into the Department of Motor Vehicles. You fail the eye exam. You flunk the written exam, and the road test is a disaster. You are denied a renewal of your license. You leave depressed and feeling like a helpless child.

Remember when you couldn't wait to turn 18, and the time when you started to hide your age? What made the difference?

A friend shared this little ditty:

> As a rule a man's a fool.
> When it's hot, he wants it cool.
> When it's cool, he wants it hot.
> Always wanting what is not.

I've tried to live by a philosophy that seems to work. Every day of my boyhood I looked forward to adventure. I entered college with high hopes of enjoying every class. My first day as a minister was thrilling. I put on my new black suit, black tie, and black shoes (that's what my major professor said to do), and began visiting the parishioners. I always thrived on trying something new. I approached retirement as an opportunity to expand my horizons. I decided that life is a gift from God, and I would live it with zest.

Being around older people who spend most of their time grousing about their chronic ailments, aches, and pains is unbearable to me. The worst situation is getting stuck with people who live in the past. That often happens while I'm waiting in the barbershop and the car repair shop.

The prophet Isaiah brought these words from God to Judah: "Do not remember the former things, or consider the things of old. I am about to do a new thing; now it springs forth, do you not perceive it?" (Isa. 43:18, 19, NRSV).

Life is for anticipating the future and creatively experiencing the present. I met a man who still believed that at 80 years of age. He was planning to go to Oshkosh, Wisconsin, to participate in the annual air show. He had been a fighter pilot in his military days, crashed and walked away from two private planes, and parachuted many times. Now he was going to hang glide, a sport he had enjoyed for many years. Instead of jumping off cliffs, he was now being towed to nearly 3,000 feet. After being released from the tow plane, he soared as long as possible before landing on a grass landing strip. He was being booked as the oldest hang glider pilot (a 12-year-old girl was booked as the youngest). When asked if he was scared when the tow plane released him, he said, "It was too late to be scared."

The Old Testament tells about 80-year-old Barzillai, who fed King David's army while under pursuit from Absalom. The king wanted to honor him for his outstanding accomplishment by taking him to live in the royal palace, but Barzillai said, What have I done to deserve such an honor? At 80 he considered such deeds as nothing out of the ordinary. He looked at life as a chance to live life to the fullest. That included doing for others what obviously needed to be done.

I've lived long enough to learn that taking counsel from young and old can get me down the pike a lot farther than trying to do it on my own. I was trying to print more than one copy of a document at a time, but I could not figure out how to do it. My 10-year-old grandson was standing nearby. He saw my predicament and snapped off a few instructions. In moments my printer was clicking off multiple copies.

I spent the night in the home of a 90-year-old Amish couple in Kansas. I had to leave at 4 a.m. for my journey home. I told them not to stir when I left, but when I headed for the front door at four, the husband met me with a flashlight to show me safely down the stairs and to my car. Sleep in? Not when you have a guest leaving at four. He taught me a lesson in hospitality. He was living in the present.

A college roommate of mine sang a little jingle that went something like this, "I wish I was single again. I wish I was single again. If I was single, my pockets would jingle. Oh, I wish I was single again."

Life is not for looking back even if our pockets are empty. Life is for filling every moment of the present in such a way that God can use us however He sees fit.

PEDAL TO THE METAL?

Back in Model-T days my father's uncle Will enjoyed the scenery while his nephews drove his car. He preferred my father's manner of driving, because my father accelerated slowly from a stop. Uncle Will believed rapid acceleration from a stop wasted gasoline.

My father drilled that concept into my mind as I learned to drive. It has saved me from high stress levels and high fuel expenses.

While a mechanic was changing the oil in my car, I chatted in the waiting room with another customer who owned the same model car as mine. When I told him I got 33 miles per gallon, he told me he only got 26. I shared my acceleration theory with him, but he didn't seem convinced. He maintained that he bought a defective car and vowed to trade it in on a new model.

I'm always amused when a sports car driver pulls next to me at a red light. When the light turns green he squeals his tires only to meet me at the next light. It reminds me of the Pennsylvania Dutch saying, "The hurrieder I go, the behinder I get."

I once traveled with a hospital CEO who impatiently ran from one airport counter to another to find an earlier flight. Then we ran down terminal halls to breathlessly board a plane just before the doors closed. He seemed to enjoy the adventure, but the insane rush to save 30 minutes caused me much stress. I preferred a layover and a chance to chat with a fellow traveler.

Two motorcyclists flew past my sons and I as we backpacked in Michigan's Pigeon River Country State Forest. Only a few minutes later they returned, announcing, "The trail ends up there. We didn't see a trail marker anywhere." Unaffected by their announcement, we kept walking. At the place they turned around we walked into the woods and found the marker. An hour later we arrived at the trail head in time to see them loading their cycles into a pickup truck. "How did you guys get here?" they asked. "Oh, we followed the trail markers," we answered. They had gone by too fast to notice them.

Dr. James J. Lynch spent years studying hypertension. He noticed that blood pressure levels dropped when people spoke and walked more slowly. When we hurry, adrenalin surges through our system, causing a state of alert. Dr. Archibald Hart states that the hurriers actually become addicted to their own adrenalin. When life slows down, they suffer withdrawal symptoms. They need an adrenalin fix, so they quickly find a way to increase the frenzy in their day.

Jesus knew the importance of slowing the pace. He and his disciples were pressed by the crowds, but Jesus took his men to a quiet place to rest, to recuperate from the hectic pace.

I have an idea that Jesus subscribed to the homey advice, "Take time to smell the roses."

There's a lot of sound religion in putting the brakes on the rapid pace of our modern high-tech world.

HOSPITALITY

Our neighbors called to say they were bringing supper on Wednesday. My wife set the table with a fancy tablecloth and her special dishes. We brought toys from the basement to occupy their children.

A few minutes before seven they came with a potato casserole, fresh peas, and a salad. For dessert they brought cookies and freshly churned homemade ice cream. We adults enjoyed conversation while the children played with the toy garage.

A year ago our family gathered for the Christmas holiday. There were 12 of us. Our neighbors, who have 10 children, decided to have all of us for a meal. We arrived to find baked casseroles and heaped-up bowls of vegetables adorning the table, which stretched almost the entire length of their large kitchen. For dessert they passed large bowls of homemade ice cream and baked delicacies.

Our friends Herb and Treva Swarm operate a bed and breakfast called The Bee Hive. The usual bed and breakfast provides a place to sleep and a small breakfast before you leave. Not at The Bee Hive. When we arrive in the early afternoon, Treva has left a note on the door: "Come in. Make yourself at home. Your room is the last one on the left. Be back soon."

We usually eat supper at a small restaurant, then return to the country for the evening. About seven or eight o'clock Herb straps on his accordion and begins playing hymns. The guests gather, and we sing. Sometimes Herb plays the wrong refrain for a hymn, which sets everyone laughing. After a half a dozen songs, Herb spins yarns that are only half believable and quite humorous. When Treva thinks Herb is carrying his tales too far, she invites everyone to sit around the long table for tea, cookies, and ice cream.

In the morning we wake to the aroma of Treva's breakfast casserole, fresh muffins, and many other good smells. Everyone gathers around the table for a feast. Treva urges every guest to eat their fill.

When Herb finishes eating, he leans back in his chair and spins more yarns. Nobody thinks of checkout time. The hospitality is too good to leave.

After the barn burned down on the farm my father sharecropped for years, we moved 50 miles south to a village called Peach Bottom. We had no church nearby, but a single mother held church in her living room every week. She was busy raising her children, but that did not keep her from entertaining. She frequently urged us to stay for a meal. I still remember the taste of her blackberry sunken, a deep dish pie. We ate it with cold goat milk, for a treat far surpassing the fanciest gourmet feast.

In Hawaii we stayed in a guesthouse overlooking the ocean. We had our own kitchen for meal preparation. Every morning the owner brought a dish of fresh pineapple or other fruit from his garden. He played soothing music on his large stereo while we ate. He and his wife often joined us for friendly chats about island history.

In a book about Old Testament customs I learned that it was traditional to set up a symbol by the doorway at mealtime to signify to passing strangers that they were welcome to share a meal. That's hospitality par excellence!

My mother used to jokingly say that she could always add a little water to the soup. She never added water, but she always had plenty for a guest who showed up at mealtime.

I invited a husband/wife team who hosted a TV show to speak at the church where I was the pastor. I also told them that they would have dinner with us. When they arrived there were seven of them, not two.

Because my wife is an excellent lip reader, I told her from the rostrum that she had to feed seven instead of two. She didn't hear a word of the sermon that day. She was planning how to make a meal for six stretch to feed 13.

She seated our four sons in the kitchen and gave them a simple, quick meal with a promise to make their favorites the next day. She and I agreed to take very small helpings. Thanks to a couple guests who were dieting, we had enough to suffice. Forced hospitality? Not really. We were happy and honored to meet their needs before they returned to New York City.

At the time of our thirty-fifth wedding anniversary my wife and I were returning from a seven-week itinerary in the Far East. We planned a four-day stopover in Hawaii, but told the guesthouse owner that we were not sure exactly when we'd arrive. He told me to call when we reached Honolulu. When I called he told me his rooms were all taken. Then he said, "Listen, why don't you come? My wife and I will sleep on the family-room floor with our grandchildren. They'll love it." We slept in comfort, thanks to people who knew how to be hospitable.

Our Lord was born in a stable because there wasn't room for one more. I often wonder if the innkeeper could not have found a little space for a pad for the weary couple.

I hope we have room for Jesus in the inn of our life. What a pity it would be to turn Him away. What an honor to offer Him hospitality!

IT TAKES TIME

"Come with me," the camp director ordered. "We're going to have a treat ready for the kiddies when they come to camp."

I followed him to the weather-beaten barn. In one of the hay lofts I saw the old rowboat. It had not touched water in many years. Gaping cracks and warped gunwales screamed of long neglect, but the director sounded like the founder of the local optimist club. Rolls of heavy cord and containers of caulk fell from his shopping bag as he mumbled directions for filling the cracks. We set to work, stuffing the cord in the cracks and smoothing on the caulk. For three days we patched the old boat and finally applied two coats of bright red paint.

The camp director was as eager to launch it as the builders of the *Queen Elizabeth II*. We lifted it onto a flatbed trailer and transported it to the lake. Gently we slipped it into the water, pushing it out a few feet while I held the rope attached to it. We proudly watched it float. "They'll love it," the director said excitedly. "She's a real winner, don't you think."

I agreed as I continued admiring the vessel. As I watched, the boat seemed to be resting lower in the water. The worst was happening right before our eyes. In a matter of 10 minutes the red beauty sank beneath the ripples on the lake. The director mumbled a few words of explanation and ordered me to pull it to shore. With great effort we tipped it over and loaded it on the trailer. We returned it to its home of many years, never to be touched or mentioned again.

Many years later I visited a boat-building establishment on Little Cranberry Island off the rocky coast of Maine The master craftsman was skillfully building a dory. "How long," I inquired, "will it take to complete this dory?"

"If all goes well, we should launch it in a year," he replied.

I could not help but think about our three-day repair job and our confidence that it would be a perfect craft.

A friend in his 60s bought a banjo and arranged to take lessons. After a few months he was still unable to play like Flatt and Scruggs. He expressed his disappointment to his teacher, who told him, "Jim, your problem is that you began playing the banjo 50 years too late. Flatt and Scruggs became famous after years of hard work and practice."

A young Baptist preacher sat next to me as we listened to a 100-year-old pastor deliver a 15-minute sermon. Without notes he read his text, expounded on it, applied it, and made the appeal. He sat down exactly 15 minutes after he began.

The Baptist leaned over and whispered to me, "I wish I could preach like that old boy." I replied, "When you study and preach as long as Oscar has, you'll be able to do the same."

I walked into the workshop of a Michigan violin maker. The floors were polished. The walls held templates and tools. An outline of each item was painted on the wall to guarantee that everything would be in place. In a glass case hung six shiny violins.

"How long have you been making violins?" I asked.

"My father was a violin maker for many years. When I was just a boy he taught me the trade, and I've built 16 violins every year for more than 25 years."

"Where do you get the wood?" I asked.

"All the wood is from mature trees, but I use only wood that has cured for years. I have wood that my father acquired years ago."

"Who will build these marvelous instruments after you retire?" I asked.

He drew a big breath and said, "I really can't answer that. I put ads in the paper offering to teach people to build violins at no charge, but I only have one student. When people learn that it takes years to learn this trade, they don't come back. My one student has been with me for a year, but I have no assurance that he'll stick it out."

Could it be that the no-tools-for-assembly age has eroded all initiative to patiently learn the skills to form works of lasting beauty? Has sermon preparation come to a mere recitation from a book— *Fifty-two Easy Sermons?* Does character development hinge on reading *Character Growth for Dummies?* Is planned obsolescence going to turn our cornfields into landfills? Whatever happened to the Bible's admonition to do whatever our hands find to do with all our might? (Ecclesiastes 9:10.)

A DEAD CAR? NO PROBLEM

A jolly young man met me and my wife at the Jakarta, Indonesia, airport. Jeff was sent to drive us to Bandung where I was scheduled to teach a group of nurses and ministers. The car he was driving appeared to be made of parts of two cars. The backseat had lost the padding. The muffler had long since blown. The roar of the diesel motor was deafening. Jeff navigated us through the jungle of cars, busses, trucks, motorcycles, various horse-drawn vehicles, and bicycle taxis.

As we began ascending the mountains, I smelled a hot oil odor that told me the engine had overheated. We stopped at a mountain-top restaurant for lunch. When we boarded the car again the motor barely turned over. We pulled into the hospital parking lot as the hot smell worsened.

After my classes ended, Jeff decided that we needed to drive to Jakarta the evening before our plane was to leave. I watched as he poured gallons of water into the radiator, but he didn't check the oil level. We quickly tossed our bags into the trunk, and Jeff sped out toward the road to Jakarta. As the car climbed the mountain I saw vapor coming out of the air conditioner vents. The vapor smelled like burning oil. I said to Jeff, "Jeff, it smells like your engine is over-heating." He tromped on the gas as he yelled, "No problem."

In Jakarta Jeff attempted to take us to a mission compound, but the gate at the entrance was locked. The night watchman was not around, so Jeff climbed over the gate and went in search. Fifteen minutes later he vaulted over the fence without the watchman. He drove to a fancy hotel, but apparently decided that staying there would be too expensive.

Jeff drove us to the opposite side of the city and stopped in front of a pastor's home. He went into the house and came out 10 min-utes later to invite us into the home for the night The pastor's wife showed us to a bedroom with a bed with only a sheet over the mat-tress. We did not think to ask the location of the bathroom. Our main interest was sleep. A few hours after retiring we urgently needed to find the bathroom. After entering an occupied bedroom and a closet, we managed to find it. Shortly after falling asleep, Jeff awakened us to go to the airport.

Without checking oil or water, Jeff started the motor, and we jumped into the backseat. The farther we drove the louder the engine rattled. I kept saying, "Jeff, this motor is going to burn up." His reply was always, "No problem." We paid toll at the entrance to the airport freeway and quickly gained speed, but not for long. The engine lost power, faltered, and made a loud noise. Jeff pulled to the shoulder of the road just as the engine stopped. He pushed the starter over and over again, but not a sputter came from the engine. Jeff jumped out of the car and opened the hood. I ran to his side saying, "Jeff, the engine is ruined. It will not start again." "No problem," was his reply.

I insisted that we flag down a bus so that we would not miss our flight. He finally agreed. The second bus stopped, and we climbed aboard with our luggage. The bus driver charged us much more than the normal fare, but I was happy to be headed to the airport. As the bus turned back on to the highway, I glanced back at Jeff and his dead car. He was continuing to labor over the car that would never run again.

I shared this event with a man who spent years in Jakarta. He told me that it is not unusual to see dead cars along the road because the drivers seem to think that cars can run without oil. Maintenance is frequently ignored.

Such drivers are not without company. I spent 14 years in hospitals, where I met patients who lived with little regard for their bodies. They ate too much, drank heavily, and filled their lungs with nicotine and tar for years. When their bodies rebelled and disease was far advanced, they couldn't understand why it happened to them. They had repeatedly said "No problem" to life's warnings, and now they faced death. They were left pushing the starter button, but there was no response from the starter.

CHAPTER 4

Growing in Christ

BEARS—ADDICTED?

As I cruised the Trans-Canada Highway through Glacier National Park, I suddenly saw a huge black bear loping from the forest onto the highway. I slammed on my brakes, as did the oncoming motorists. The bear nimbly turned in the center of the road and returned to the safety of the forest.

I had struck two deer in Michigan, killing both instantly, with minimum damage to my car. I dreaded thinking about the damage a bear would inflict on the thin sheet metal and fiberglass of my car.

A few miles down the road I stopped at a visitors' center. I told the gift shop manager about my bear encounter. He said, "Oh, yes. Bears in the spring go crazy over dandelion. When they have dandelion on the brain they couldn't care less about danger on the highway. Frequently we get reports of bear killed on the road in springtime."

Bears are addicted to dandelion, and they risk death in pursuit of this bitter herb.

Humans are similar. I've visited cancer patients in oncology units who desperately crave a cigarette. The very substance that brought them to the brink of death is the driving thought captivating them. With the doctor's prognosis still ringing in their ears, they reach for a "smoke" and light up.

I met a man who violated the law and verbally abused police officers when he sniffed glue. He was in and out of prison repeatedly, but the thought of glue overcame all pleas from his family

I had to work as a hospital orderly for 10 days as part of chaplaincy training. My first patient was a young man who loved to ride Harleys at breakneck speed. Now he lay in bed with a broken leg. The swelling in the leg made the skin appear ready to split. As the physical therapist and I assisted him in his morning walk, the therapist asked him if he had his fill of speed. "Are you kidding?" he responded. "I have a new Harley in the crate in my garage. It has more power than the one I wrecked. I can't wait to take that baby on the turnpike."

I can easily sit in judgment on these people because I'm not addicted to speed, tobacco, or glue. Addiction to dandelion greens isn't a problem either. (My mother cooked them every spring and insisted I eat them as a spring tonic. Ever since I left home I have not had a spring tonic.)

Yet I can easily destroy myself with anger, worry, resentment, and a mean spirit. These kinds of things can get a grip on me that destroys my relationship with God and others. I can continue harboring damaging attitudes, even when I know they put me in jeopardy of losing eternal life.

The apostle Paul wrote about the death grip of behaviors that were as repulsive as carrying a corpse on your back. Joyfully he declared that deliverance from the shackles of any sin comes from the power of God.

After conducting a smoking cessation program I received a

phone call from one of the successful participants. He was in the hospital for elective surgery and asked me to visit. What he said taught me a profound lesson.

"Larry, you and the doctor had your medical and psychological information well in hand. You were very convincing. When you spoke about spiritual help in breaking the smoking habit, you soft-pedaled that information. I'm of the Jewish faith. I asked you to visit me because you need to know that the power of God broke the hold tobacco had on my life. My advice to you is, Don't soft pedal the spiritual tools in breaking bad habits."

I don't know about breaking a bear's addiction to dandelion, but using my Jewish friend's advice, I have seen many people celebrating victory over life-shrinking lifestyles.

The Bible says that we can do all things through Christ who strengthens us. The flow of power is abundant. It requires that by God's grace we acknowledge our inability to change and open our souls to the flow of His power.

HEAVENLY TRANSLATOR

I walked through a small village in the beautiful island country of Dominican Republic. A friendly man tried to hold a conversation with me, but I did not speak Spanish, and his English was extremely limited. With the aid of hand motions and body language I was able to understand that he and his wife had ten children, his wife was visiting the dentist, the rain was making his garden grow well, and God was good to him. Finally, in Spanish he said, "In Spanish you are very deficient. In English I am very deficient." He then shook my hand and wished me a good day.

In the little town of Jarabacoa, Dominican Republic, I went to the store to buy postcards. All my made-up words could not convey what I needed to the store owner. My helplessness in a Spanish speaking country was overwhelming.

In both cases I needed a translator like the one I had in Mexico. He was fluent in both Spanish and English. He not only translated words, but used all the voice inflections and gestures that I used.

Have you ever felt as if you needed a translator when you pray? Have you ever been so choked up with emotion that words would not come out? Were you ever at a loss for words to express the enormity of the problem? Did you wonder if you were getting through? I have good news for you.

God doesn't expect perfect diction or elocution style. It doesn't matter if you stutter, stammer, or stumble. God reads the language of the heart. The Holy Spirit translates our longings into the language of heaven. The message goes through loud and clear.

Dr. James J. Lynch wrote three books about loneliness. He emphasizes the need for dialogue. The largest percentage of dialogue is nonverbal. An elderly couple may know each other's thoughts without speaking. If bonded human beings can understand each other nonverbally, certainly God can understand us without our uttering a word. It doesn't matter if I verbalize my thoughts in Spanish, French, or Greek. God reads our heart.

During 26 years as a hospice chaplain, I have watched many families stand by the bed of a terminally ill loved one. They touch, smile, and sometimes speak very little, yet one message is clearly sent: I love you.

Can God do the same? I think so. Standing at His trial, Jesus simply looked at the denying disciple Peter. That look showed love and pity. This drove Peter, weeping, to his place of confession and repentance.

When I perform a wedding ceremony, my favorite part is when the couple face each other during the vows and during the vocal solo after they are pronounced husband and wife. The intensity of emotion shown through their eyes cannot be verbalized. The love message is clearly understood by both.

The Holy Spirit speaks to us about many things as we walk through life. He does not use a loud, audible voice that booms at our ear drums. He speaks in a still, small voice heard only in the soul. It convicts, teaches, reminds, and assures us of God's love.

Isn't it exciting to know that the Holy Spirit not only translates for us, but also speaks to us? His communication leaps over all language barriers. He is our heavenly translator.

LESSONS FROM HOBOS

The Great Depression of 1929 left lingering negative effects on society. Joblessness was one of the more serious problems. Young men and old men roamed the countryside doing odd jobs and asking for food.

My family's farm was a prime destination for these hobos because a railroad ran along the edge of our pasture. They often jumped the train in town and jumped off as the train slowed as it approached the little town of Cornwall. They walked back on the tracks and stopped at our place.

Their clothes were tattered, their shoes sometimes reinforced with cardboard fastened to the soles of their shoes with cords. Their long hair and bushy beards frightened me at age 6 or 7. When I saw a hobo shuffling up the farm lane, I'd hide under the low branches of a weeping willow tree.

A blue-eyed Irishman with a grinder on his back always coaxed me out of hiding. I helped him clamp his grinder to the barnyard gate, then he asked me to bring knives, scissors, sickles, and scythes to be sharpened. I turned the handle of the grinder while he skillfully sharpened. After I returned the sharpened items to their places, he rapped on the farmhouse door.

"Madam, would you be willing to give a hungry man a bite to eat?" he'd ask my mother. She never turned away a hobo who was willing to work.

My father left a fallen tree in the meadow. We called it the hobo tree. If a hobo did not bring some service to our door, my folks invited him to cut and split a wheelbarrow load of firewood before receiving a meal. They believed in working for your keep.

My father invited one young hobo to live with us as a hired hand. He was given new shoes and clothes. He slept in the barn at his request. He helped with the milking and fieldwork. After a few months he quietly left in the night.

For years I wondered why so many hobos visited our farm. I learned that they left signals on road signs and telephone poles that noted the degree of hospitality that could be expected. My mother's chicken potpie and raisin pie was known throughout hobodom.

Since my boyhood on the farm I have been saddened by the beggars who have approached me with outstretched hands in poverty-stricken lands. On a recent trip to Mexico, an elderly woman came toward me as I was leaving a church. With her hands over her heart, she looked into my face intently without uttering a word. All my attempts to communicate brought nothing but her pitiful stare.

I reached in my pocket and handed her a U.S. dollar. My friend took the dollar from her hand and gave her a Mexican bill worth twice as much. "There! Now we have both helped her," she said. The beggar shuffled away, content with her gift.

Isn't it strange that people in need are willing to face rejection and humiliation to gain material things from fellow humans, yet there are people who hesitate to ask God for material or spiritual blessings. On the other hand, there are people who confidently ask God for help and report amazing replies. They don't consider it begging. They ask because they know that God is interested in their affairs.

An old man in Lebanon, Pennsylvania, told me his experience from the Great Depression. He and his wife crawled into bed one cold night. She expressed concern about making breakfast when the cupboards were bare. They slipped out of bed and knelt on the cold floor to ask God to help them.

The next morning they discovered bags of groceries on their porch. Their cupboards were full again, but they never knew where the groceries came from.

My goal is to trust God implicitly the way my first son did when he was only 4. My wife noticed him kneeling in the backyard with a neighbor girl. When he entered the house she asked, "What were you doing in the back yard?"

"I lost my quarter. We were asking Jesus to help us find it," he answered.

"Did you find it?" she asked.

"Of course, Mom!" he confidently replied.

That's the kind of trust I pray for.

COUNTING THE COST

Five-year-old David was climbing a tree with his older brothers. He stood on a limb halfway up, but he was too short to reach the branch above him. Not to be outdone by his brothers, he jumped as high as he could and grabbed the branch. The branch snapped and David fell to the ground . . . breaking one arm and his jaw.

For the next month he walked with his arm in a sling and drank his food through a straw. He learned the hard way not to grab things that won't support you.

Ed had just received his first driver's license. His friends were driving cars to school, so Ed decided he'd spend his savings on a car. His budget was limited, so he went to a used car lot that advertised affordable prices. There he saw a car with a price tag that matched his resources. Without doing any research on the reliability of that car, he signed the papers and parted with his cash.

Most of the time his car wouldn't run. When it did run, it was loud and slow. Ed was the laughingstock of his school friends.

David and Ed learned that being too hasty to keep up with others can be disappointing, and even disastrous.

Jesus talked about a contractor who built his house on sand. The flash floods came in the rainy season and his house crumbled. He obviously didn't do his research before he built.

When I was looking for a house to buy in a small Texas town, I was warned about buying a house where a fault line ran through. Dozens of people had built homes there against the advice of long-time residents. Their walls cracked, and their driveways buckled. Reselling was very difficult.

Deciding to jump, buy, or build can be puzzling and disappointing.

My sons spent hours discussing careers with me. In most cases they had qualifications to do a number of things. College professors tried to interest them in their disciplines, which made the decision more complex. That was years ago. Today technology is changing so rapidly that it is possible to decide on one career and find it obsolete at the time of graduation.

A young person needs to do much research and much praying for guidance in career decisions. Leaping on a hunch can lead to wasted time and discouragement.

As I sat in the barber chair a young man came to chat with the barber, asking about the legal requirements for opening a gun shop. The barber wished him well, but told him that since the Brady Bill the government was closing large numbers of gun shops. Regulations were getting tougher.

When the young man left, I asked the barber about him. "Well, he is a good-hearted kid who would give you the shirt off his back, but he can't find his niche in life. He worked in a bank for three months, but that fell through. He earned his real estate license, but the market was flooded with agents, so that failed. He's now working in a restaurant, but he's not a good fit for the job. Now he's thinking about opening a gun shop."

I bought my first car from a fellow college student. He purchased the car from an older man who seldom drove it. After a short courtship he proposed to a girl who initially said Yes, but after he bought the car she broke the engagement. The car held memories and broken plans in his mind, so he sold it.

After studying for the gospel ministry for four years, he realized that his career decision was made because some people in his church told him he'd make a good minister. After four years he carefully examined the decision he'd made on the recommendations of others. He decided to stay in college and finish a degree in business. This time he decided wisely.

Jesus said you shouldn't proceed with a project until you sit down and calculate the cost. (See Luke 14:28.)

Calculating the cost in today's world requires advice and insight from experienced counselors. It requires help in determining your strengths. It requires a close walk with God and a sincere prayer, "Show me, Lord, the direction in which you'd like me to go."

A NEW HORSE

Bill Coleman's father was the village blacksmith. Town folk often dropped in to share news and a little gossip. The town drunk was a frequent visitor. The blacksmith didn't seem disturbed by his slurred speech and chronic complaints about his wife.

One day the inebriated visitor led his bag-of-bones horse to the shop. He was out of money and booze, so he offered to sell his horse to the blacksmith for $20. The deal was closed, and the smithy took the horse home to be rehabilitated.

Once the horse was in prime condition, the blacksmith rode it to work. The drunk came by when he had money in his pocket. Seeing the sleek horse tied to the hitching post, the drunk asked the blacksmith, "How much for that handsome horse? I need a horse like that for getting about."

The offer was $200. The drunk paid and rode the horse home. A week later he came to the shop.

"A curious thing happened," reported the drunk. "That horse you sold me went into the barn with no trouble. That's not all. It went into the same stall my old horse occupied."

When the blacksmith revealed the identity of the horse, the drunk protested. "You charged me $200 for the horse you paid me $20 for. That's outrageous."

"Oh, no," said the blacksmith. "I fed your horse $200 worth of good feed to restore it to good health. You paid for your own neglect."

The Bible says we reap what we sow. If we don't care for our car, we pay a big repair bill. If we overeat we suffer from obesity. If we fill our lungs with smoke, we lose a lung. If we allow our house to fall into disrepair, we lose money on resale.

I heard the distinct sound of a vintage automobile as I walked around Fredericksburg, Texas. An old Oldsmobile with many cylinders pulled into a service station. A young man was chauffeuring the elderly lady sitting next to him. He pumped 16 gallons of gas into the tank. When the owner scrutinized the receipt, she exclaimed, "Sixteen gallons? Son, this car doesn't take that much gas." The chauffeur reached into the glove box and extracted an owner's manual that looked as if it just came off the press. He turned to the specifications page and proved that the tank held 20 gallons.

The chauffeur told me the car was always kept in the garage and driven only to go on necessary errands. Driven or not, it was wiped down with polishing cloths every day. I stood by the car until the engine was started. It purred.

Many similar cars have rusted away many years ago. This one was sought after because the owner was a good steward

A farm located a few miles from my home used to be the envy of local farmers. The buildings were nicely painted and the crops were the best. Lawns were mowed neatly, and flower and vegetable gardens were weedless. Now the original owners cannot bear to drive by the place. The barn is sagging, and the outbuildings are falling down. The lawns have turned to mud thanks to hundreds of roaming ducks. Piles of old lumber are visible everywhere. If the present owner decides to sell, he will take a drastic loss on his investment

Jesus talked about a man who was given money to use wisely. He buried it and didn't put it to good use. Another man invested his money and was able to show his master a good return.

God gives each of us abilities, skills, talents. Some people hide and even abuse them. Some use them to bring joy to others. The difference is found in their connection with the Bestower of the gifts.

My son and I attended a performance of the Fort Worth Symphony Orchestra. The guest artist was a renowned guitarist. Before he performed he told the audience that he had not played or recorded for several years because life had seemed empty and without purpose. But he had recently accepted Jesus as his personal Savior, and life had taken on a whole new dimension. Now he is using his music to bless others.

The sound system was not working for the first few bars of his music. He stopped the orchestra until the system functioned so that we could hear the entire composition. The audience applauded with delight.

God in our life makes us good stewards of time, talent, means, health, and property. We receive wisdom from Him to sow in a manner that guarantees a rewarding yield.

NEVER STOP GROWING

My wife was decorating our living room and setting the dining room table when Tammy, our 5-year-old neighbor, walked in. "What are you doing?" she asked.

"I'm getting ready for a birthday party. Our friend, Mr. Smith, is 100 years old."

Tammy rolled her eyes and said, "Oh boy, he must be *real* big!"

A little girl who is told how big she is getting at every birthday would have reason to think that 100 birthdays would increase one's physical stature exponentially.

Children have great interest in growing. Names, inch marks, and dates decorate one of our closet walls. Every visit brings requests to be measured. Our grandchildren go to school and report the latest figures to their classmates.

I've met people in their later years who complain about growing shorter. It seems to be inevitable with aging, but it is contrary to our way of thinking. Our childhood idea of ongoing physical growth is difficult to erase.

I visited a health club in Canada and watched Mr. Canada working out on free weights. Other young men were pumping iron in the weight room, aspiring to one day take the title. Growing in muscle strength has been the dream of many youth.

As a young man I was no exception. I aspired to become like Charles Atlas, the idol of that era. Standing in front of a mirror, I flexed my muscles, trying to convince myself that I was well on my way to becoming a hulk.

One of my college roommates walked up and down the halls on his hands to increase the size of his upper body. Another roommate had me stand on his abdomen to increase the strength of his stomach muscles.

What about the desire for spiritual growth? Does that equal the interest in physical growth?

A youth leader asked me to attend the youth Bible class to participate in a panel discussion. It was held in the same chapel where I was a youth leader 25 years before. Back then we had more youth in the halls than in the chapel. Now it was different. The chapel was nearly full. The youth asked their peers to pray for serious matters. They engaged in discussion and planned to create a drama for an upcoming worship service.

A friend who works at a university told me about a unique worship opportunity created by students. They developed a number of stations where students can sing, read Scripture, meditate, create religious art, or discuss issues of the spiritual life. They come by the hundreds and stay until nearly midnight.

My son has directed many two and three week mission trips to third world countries. The youth who go with him lay blocks, mix mortar, dig trenches, and swing paint brushes, but they do more. They gather groups of children for singing and Bible stories. They help the sick along with a medical or dental professional. Before returning to the United States they give away much of their clothing. Their passion for helping others is living testimony to their love for God.

Growth in height and muscular bulk may have stopped, but there is evidence of a growing spirituality among the young.

HE LOVES ME—FEELINGS AND ALL

Jesus stood by the grave of his friend Lazarus and bawled. The tears of divinity mingled with the tears of humanity. Lazarus' sisters Mary and Martha knew He had entered into their sorrow.

Jesus stood by the empty grave and embraced those three siblings. The laughter and rejoicing of divinity mingled with the laughter and rejoicing of humanity.

What a swing of emotions happened on that day. Jesus was swept up in all of them.

Children were drawn to Jesus because He could shed tears when they skinned a knee, and He could laugh when they turned a somersault. Children can travel from heartbreaking sobs to laughter in a moment. The full spectrum of emotions can appear and disappear like a rainbow. Jesus loved them no matter where they were in their emotional roller coaster.

A preacher entered the hospital room where a parishioner had just died. He took one look at the weeping family and chastised them for weak faith.

At a church camp meeting I heard the sobs of a little child who became separated from her mother. Several adults stood tall over her and assured her that her mother would soon be back. Not wanting her to suffer any longer, I swooped down and picked her up in my arms. "There now," I comforted. "You and I will go looking for your mama."

Her tears began to diminish. Soon her mother saw her in my arms. In a moment she was in her mother's arms, crying harder than ever. Her mother was crying with her. How sweet the shared tears. They were followed by wiping and the gradual return of smiles of relief.

God is like that mother. He joins us in our sorrow and celebrates our joy.

Burl Ives sang a song that said laughter is a funny way of crying. It seems to me that masking tears with laughter indicates a fear of showing true emotions, perhaps fear of being rejected if our real emotions showed.

That's what I like about God. He takes me as I am. I don't have to hide my feelings because I know He already knows what they are. I know He accepts me in my tears and in my laughter.

I have had difficulty expressing my feelings to people. I like to blame it on my Pennsylvania Dutch heritage, but that's not fair. Fear of what others would think of me is probably the most likely reason.

When I was a boy, I crawled under the covers with my brown

teddy bear. There in the darkness I poured my sorrows and my dreams to that shabby stuffed cloth. When my sisters teased me for making funny faces due to a nervous tic, I escaped to the barn to cry.

At 41 years of age, I enrolled in a chaplaincy training program. My supervisors accused me of hiding my feelings. During my final evaluation before three supervisors I was subjected to relentless accusations of being unfeeling. All at once I broke into uncontrollable sobbing, but I couldn't utter a word of explanation. They ended the interview abruptly. I left the room feeling broken and misunderstood.

I have never felt that way with God. Sometimes while writing a sermon or a book chapter, I feel what I am writing so deeply that I weep. I never hide those tears from God. I feel His comfort like warm arms around me. I feel healing and understanding.

My wife is the greatest blessing God has given me. Whenever I weep from sorrow, her arms are instantly around me. She becomes the personification of how God responds. Her heart is filled with love, and comfort spills into my broken heart.

The apostle Paul told the Corinthian Christians that when we are sad God gives us overflowing comfort. You don't have to hide your feelings from God. He makes it so safe to share. His comfort exceeds all your needs.

DO ANGELS CRY?

Children streamed down the center aisle of the church. There were shepherds garbed in bathrobes, wise men wrapped in gaudy fabric, and three angels equipped with wings and halos. Three played the piano and keyboards as the children told the Christmas story. There could be no pauses because the scripted music prompted the various speakers.

The bathrobed shepherds acted afraid when a bright light shone on the stage and the three little angels appeared to proclaim, "Don't be afraid. We bring you good news of great joy. You will find a baby wrapped in swaddling clothes and lying in a manger. Glory to God. Peace on earth. Good will to men."

Each of the three angels had a third of the lines. The first two spoke clearly and confidently, but the third angel stood speechless before the microphone. She danced from one foot to the other, but she could not recall her line. The pianos played the music for the next scene, leaving the cute, curly-haired angel numb with fear. Realizing she had missed her chance to finish the angel announcement, she puckered up and wept. The littlest angel cried while the pageant continued.

Do angels cry? I hope so. We lose a dear loved one and the world rushes on. We feel alone and forgotten. Wouldn't it help to believe that angels cry with us?

In a dark, war-torn, troubled world of suicide bombings, smart bombs, child abuse, and rampant pornography, surely the angels long to announce eternal joy and peace. They stand poised to shout their lines, but the brutality and unthinkable atrocities escalate. Surely the tears flow down angelic faces at the sight of continuing tragedy. A tear-soaked world must prompt weeping in heavenly realms.

Oh yes, I forgot to tell you that I saw the weeping angel at the refreshment hall after the pageant. She was eating a big chocolate chip cookie. Her face beamed with a smile. What a change!

A time of refreshing for real angels will soon come. They will accompany Jesus when He returns to take His children to His eternal land, where tears will never flow. There will be no weeping angels there, because all the lines will have been fulfilled.

In the meantime, I'm glad angels still weep with me.

NO WAY TO WIPE THE TEARS

I had just finished my lecture at a university in Mexico when the new chaplain of the hospital rushed to the podium. "Can you come with me right now to conduct a funeral?" he asked.

On the short trip to the hospital, the chaplain told me that a baby was stillborn in the maternity ward. The parents wanted to have a funeral service before the infant was cremated.

I met the father at the hospital morgue. The attendant gave him a small box in which the infant was wrapped in a blanket. The father carried it to his wife's room where the two of them cried together. In a few minutes the grandparents entered the room to grieve with them. After they had a chance to talk and cry, I entered the room with friends and family.

The room was poorly furnished. The weather was sweltering, but no air-conditioning cooled the air. Without any preparation I spoke to the parents and family. I prayed and shared Bible promises with them. I stepped to the side of the bed and saw the mother's eyes filled with tears. I looked around the room for tissue, but found none. I longed to wipe her tears, but I had to stand there and watch them spill over her cheeks. I held her hand, stroked her sweating brow, and quietly prayed for her. I left her room with the longing to wipe her tears unfulfilled.

I believe God was in that hot room with me. He also longed to wipe away her tears. He sends His Spirit of comfort to help grieving mothers and fathers, but He knows the day and hour when He will dry every tear.

I have stood by the caskets of hundreds of people and watched their families tremble and weep before the lid is closed. My heart aches for every person who drops their tears on the white satin casket liner.

In my helplessness I say to myself, "He will wipe away all tears from their eyes. There will be no more sorrow nor crying."

After the resurrection I will never rush to the side of a heartsick mother. I will trade my funeral-conducting skills for the eternal pleasure of learning the secrets of life in the land where all is peace.

MAN OF SORROWS

For three years a mother came to the neonatal intensive care unit of the hospital to watch her tiny infant struggle for life. She touched her by thrusting her hands into long socks on either side of the specialized crib, but holding her baby in her arms was not an option. The baby's condition changed frequently, which sent the mother's emotions up and down like a yo-yo. Sometimes she was sure she would take her baby home. Other times she feared the whole episode would end in a funeral. After three years of hoping, her baby died.

At the funeral her pastor began the service with a jubilant smile and a booming voice. "Brothers and sisters, we have come here for a celebration! There is no reason to be sad. This little child is now in heaven, much happier than we are. We have come here to rejoice, not to cry!"

The heartbroken mother steeled herself against crying. She forced herself to think about other things so that she would show no emotion. After the funeral she climbed into her car and drove home alone, the same way she had come to the funeral.

Some of the hospital nurses were at the funeral. They were enraged at the pastor who forbid the mother to be sad. They went back to the hospital, and together with the rest of the staff came up with a plan. They would conduct a real funeral.

The next day two nurses drove to the mother's house and brought her to the hospital chapel. One by one the staff members read a poem, sang a song, or reminisced about their experience with the infant. Each of them placed a white rose at the altar. They gave the mother a chance to speak, though she had wept throughout the entire service. After the service they gathered the white roses, helped the mother into the car, and went to the cemetery to place the roses on the freshly covered grave.

A family of five stood around the bed weeping over their favorite aunt, grandmother, and mother. Their pastor entered the room dressed all dapper. He immediately took charge. "Now Auntie had 85 good years. You all need to stop the crying and praise the Lord for all the years you had her. She's with the Lord, and that should make you happy. None of this crying!"

I wonder what these pastors would have said to Jesus as He wept over the city of Jerusalem, as He wept at the tomb of Lazarus with his arms around Mary and Martha. I wonder how they feel about Jesus when they read the prophet Isaiah's picture of Jesus: "He was despised and rejected by men, a man of sorrows, and familiar with suffering" (Isa. 53:3, NIV).

How do such pastors condemn tears when the Bible says that tears won't be wiped away permanently until Jesus ushers us into His eternal kingdom? How will they handle the deaths of their own loved ones?

Compassion is the willingness to enter into the pain and sorrow of another person. It is to weep with those who weep, to grieve with those who grieve. That's what made the early Christian church such a convincing power in the pagan world.

If Jesus is called a man of sorrows, who am I to tell a fellow traveler that she should not cry? Though God never meant for us to cry in pain, tears are inevitable in this rebellious world. Jesus blended the tears of divinity with the tears of humanity. When we are sad and shed tears, we are in good company.

This is what I told a group of 38 Methodist women. All of them had lost a loved one to death, and all wept at once as I presented a lecture on adjusting to loss. I said, "I am so happy to see you crying and expressing your sorrow, not because I like to see sad people, but because you are in good company when you weep. Jesus wept. He is by your side right now to comfort and bring peace."

Tears are more than evidence of sadness. They are a testimony to the bonds of love. They are pointers to the grand reunion at the time of the promised resurrection.

Sadness? Inevitable. Permanent? Certainly not.

THE HOUSE GUEST

My sons and I noticed an Air Force plane circling the airport visible from our home in Worcester, Massachusetts. "Let's go see who is coming!" they yelled.

By the time we arrived at the airport a temporary fence was in place, and people began to gather. The boys pushed their way to the front of the line just as Vice President Gerald Ford emerged from the plane. Each of them shook his hand and received words of greeting from the high official who came to play golf for the day.

The next day Gerald Ford became the President of the United States of America. My sons boasted to their schoolmates that they had met the president.

I know the feeling. As I walked through the narrow passage way from the Capitol to the Senate Office Building in Washington, Richard Nixon was coming toward me. He stepped aside to let me pass. I shook his hand and received his cheerful greeting. That was before the disgrace of Watergate.

My family and I were leaving the Smithsonian Institution in Washington, D.C., when we saw a low-flying helicopter circling the Washington Monument. Important-looking cars with flashing lights were blocking traffic.

We ran toward the lawn next to the Washington Monument just in time to see the helicopter land. Out stepped Secretary of State Henry Kissinger.

Why were we so intrigued by people in high places? Did our meeting them somehow add to our sense of importance? Perhaps it was the novelty of the experience.

A puny tax collector with a bad reputation heard that Jesus was coming to town. He knew he would not be able to see over the heads of the crowd, so he climbed a tree. Imagine his surprise when Jesus stopped under the tree, looked up and said, "Zacchaeus, come down right now. I'm having lunch at your house today."

Can you picture Zacchaeus' wife looking out the door and seeing her husband bringing a guest? "Oh, dear. The house is a mess, and I have a pile of unfolded laundry on the best chair in the house. I haven't made anything fancy. I wish he'd tell me before inviting a colleague for lunch."

I imagine all her anxiety vanished when she looked into the kind face of Jesus. He put her at ease and made her feel important.

Jesus gave me an invitation to open my life to him. He said he'd come into my life and dine with me. He is eager to be my house guest. He knocks at your door as well. He makes no exceptions. He feels at home in the lowliest cottage and in the two million dollar condo. Open the door and your home will take on a radiance that no money can buy.

A WORK IN PROGRESS

On my way to a wedding rehearsal, my red Toyota Corolla sputtered and gasped its last, right by a Toyota dealership. I coasted into the parking lot, and the mechanic helped me push it into a service bay. In a few minutes I was on my way.

After the rehearsal I returned home by the same route. Just as I approached the Toyota dealership, the engine died. I coasted into the service area close to closing time. The mechanic discovered a clogged fuel filter. As he made the repair, he shook his head in disbelief that my car stopped twice in the same day at the same garage.

My son returned from a trip. As he drove into the parking lot at his place of employment, the transmission made a frightening noise, leaving the car inoperable. Instead of being stranded on a turnpike, he was only a mile from home.

Halfway to a professional meeting I realized I had left the address of the convention at home. How would I find it? When I arrived at O'Hare Airport my connecting flight was cancelled due to over-booking. I met a man headed for the same convention. He was cleared for the connecting flight, but he chose to give up his seat and accompany me on the next flight. He had lived in the city where the convention was being held and knew exactly how to get there. I knew I was in good hands.

Have you ever had an in-the-nick-of-time experience? Has anyone told you it was just a coincidence?

A man told me about being deathly ill and finding no doctor who could help him. One day he met a physician who specialized in the disease that had attacked his body. The physician recognized the symptoms and immediately began the treatment that saved his life.

You could never convince him that meeting the right physician was a coincidence. He believed that God had arranged the meeting.

I'm convinced that I don't initiate events in my life. God is at work on my behalf long before a situation arises. I simply fall in step with the Great Actor who has a work in progress.

The widow of Nain was trudging behind the casket of her dead son. They were headed for the cemetery, but Jesus was about to intersect her pathway. His destination was not the cemetery, but a resurrection. The widow and her son walked home together because Jesus saw ahead and provided ahead.

I know the disappointment of fishing all night without a nibble. Jesus' disciples had such a night. While they were fretting about their bad luck, Jesus was cooking fish for breakfast on the shore. He saw ahead and provided ahead.

A little fellow, perhaps on his way to his favorite fishing hole, carried a homemade lunch. On his way he was swept up by a crowd tagging along behind Jesus and his disciples. As Jesus taught the people, hunger took its toll. The disciples didn't have any ideas for feeding thousands of empty stomachs. One disciple, Andrew, saw the boy peeking into his lunch bag and inquired about its contents.

I don't think Jesus was surprised to learn about the boy's five barley loaves and two dried fish. It was simply a part of His work in progress.

Jesus knew all about Peter's cursing and denial. He had that rooster all programmed. He knew there would be a quick glance filled with shame and sorrow. He was ready with a look filled with love and forgiveness. Peter's confession and change of heart was not prompted by Peter. It was Jesus' work in progress.

If God had a prearrangement for a sick Toyota, a worn transmission, and an aimless traveler, why not a plan for your life?

When you hit detours, could God have better scenery in mind for you?

NO BETTER MACHINE

As I drove two of my Amish neighbors to a popular Amish community in Indiana, we talked about recent changes in their local church district.

"I hear the bishop has given permission to young farmers to buy and use skid loaders," I said.

"Oh, yes," said Merta. "Edward is taking delivery on one this morning. When farmers don't have sons old enough to help clean the cow barns, it takes too long, especially in the spring when there's a lot of fieldwork."

Sue piped up. "Alvin is looking for one he can afford. It won't be long before he has a new toy."

Jokingly I said, "Maybe I need to talk to the bishop and suggest that he give you ladies a time-saving device."

"You can say that again," chimed in Sue.

Merta was quiet for a long time. She broke the silence by saying, "To tell you the truth, I can't think of anything I need."

I was impressed by her contentment. I told her that the Bible says that godliness with contentment is great gain.

As I reflected on her priorities, I remembered the day I visited their home after their first baby died. I stood by the crib and looked into the face of their precious baby, then entered the living room to comfort Merta. I went into the backyard to meet the father coming in from the barn. His eyes were red from crying. We embraced as I wished him God's peace.

I understood why Merta was content with the things she possessed. Her priorities shifted when she and her husband said goodbye to their first and only daughter. Watching her life slip away caused the material things in life to fade into insignificance.

A little boy now blesses their home. Their tiny farm house is being expanded, not because they want more things, but because their growing boy needs more room to play during the cold winter months

My father bought his 80-acre farm from a very contented man. We knew him as Pappy Umberger. Aged and lame, he was unable to do farmwork. He sold and moved in with his daughter who lived in a town five miles away.

"I'll sell you the farm on one condition," Pappy told my father. "That condition is that I can come back and harvest the hazelnuts when they ripen in the fall."

True to the bargain, Pappy returned to harvest the hazelnuts, but he visited many other times as well. It was apparent to us that he had left the farm, but the farm was still in his heart.

We could tell that Pappy was coming as soon as he entered the long farm lane. He drove an old Model T Ford that rattled and coughed. My father once turned the door handle to help Pappy exit the Tin Lizzie. The handle came off in his hand. As my father replaced the handle he suggested that he might think about purchasing a newer car.

Pappy smiled and said, "I couldn't want for a better machine."

My father had just purchased a new post-war Jeep to replace his 1940 Studebaker Champion, but contented Pappy was happy with his Model-T.

Discontentment is common in our world of obsolescence. If not forced to buy new, we can easily grasp at the better model whether or not we need it.

When I visited a missionary friend in Tokyo, he showed me the nearly new TV set he had found at the landfill. The steady production of new and better devices led to the steady flow of perfectly good appliances to the dump.

I'm not a sociologist and have not read empirical studies to support what I'm about to say, but my observations make the statement seem credible. People who are content with their situation and material possessions are at peace with themselves. They are the peacemakers Jesus mentioned in the Beatitudes.

A FIERY TONGUE

"I was only 10 when my self-esteem hit rock bottom," Jennifer told me. "My parents told me that I was not their kid. They said someone dropped me on their porch, and they took me in out of pity. When I protested, they insisted it was true. They told me that for several days.

"When I became very sad and couldn't stop crying, they said 'Oh, what's the matter with you? Can't you take a joke?'"

"At 10 I believed their story. Suddenly I didn't know who I was. Try as I might, I could not shake their story, and I couldn't find out who I was."

As she choked back the tears, I asked, "You dear girl, what a horrible thing to do to a child! Did you ever discover who you are?"

"Their story destroyed all my self-esteem. I didn't think I deserved anything good in life. I fell into bad company in hopes of gaining acceptance. I married an abusive man who nearly killed me. I feared for my life and the life of my son, so I divorced him. The church I was attending kicked me out because, they said, I didn't have Bible grounds for divorce.

"That's not all," she continued. "My oldest sister died after a long and courageous struggle with cancer. Her death left me feeling adrift and alone. I couldn't bear the pain from all the loss. I did a foolish thing. I overdosed and was comatose for a week. When I awakened, a nurse told me the pastor from the church that kicked me out came to visit, but I don't remember. Since I have gotten out of the hospital, not a soul from that church has been to see me nor called to see how I'm doing."

"No wonder your self-esteem has hit rock bottom," I said.

"I lost my home, and my other sister took me into her home. She loves me like a mother—just what I've wanted all my life. I'm seeing a therapist, and she's also like a mother to me. Thanks to these two beautiful people, I'm beginning to understand who I am."

Imagine staggering through 25 years in search of your identity— all because of cruel words.

The epistle of James says the tongue can be a fire that sets on fire the course of our life. His words came true for a quarter of a century. *You're not our kid* cut deep into Jennifer's soul. Those words burned their way into her consciousness and impacted many of her decisions.

Jennifer shared her story with a support group I facilitated. I was delighted to see people swapping phone numbers with her after the group session ended. Hugs, tears, and smiles were in abundance. Words of friendship and genuine caring were undoing the damage of the cruel words spoken years earlier.

Yet the fiery tongue can be healing and nourishing when under the control of God's power.

A new mother whispers affectionate words to her tiny baby. The little eyes look intently into the mother's face and respond to the words with a tiny smile.

Newlyweds who have just exchanged vows before the minister exchange words audible only to the two of them as the vocalist sings the final song. Love shapes their expressions beyond human words to describe.

I thank my grandsons for doing yard and garage work for me. I love to watch their chests pushed out with pride and excitement. Of course, big smiles break all over their faces when I pay them the promised amount.

James said that a fountain doesn't spew out fresh and bitter water at the same time. Fig trees don't yield olives. Neither do lips controlled by God's grace speak words that hurt or embarrass. When God's power is working in us, we calculate the effect of our words before we speak them.

"Like apples of gold in settings of silver is a word spoken in right circumstances" (Prov. 25:11, NASB).

CHAPTER 5

Seeing Through Older Eyes

NOSTALGIA

Driving down a country road in Iowa, I came upon a farmer on an antique tractor slowly making his way to a nearby town. As I drove over a hill I saw dozens of tractors—John Deeres, Farmalls, Molines, Fordsons, Allis-Chalmers, Olivers, and many other makes not familiar to me.

I stopped for lunch in town. Lawn chairs lined the streets where residents would soon enjoy the tractor drive-by. After lunch I stopped at a country store. People were gathered on porches waiting for the tired irons to go by. I joined the eager spectators and counted over 100 tractors.

I longed to see a Farmall F-20 like my father had owned, on which I'd enjoyed my first solo drive at 10 years of age—pulling the disc and culti-packer in open fields to prepare the soil for planting.

An F-20 came by. I had a strong urge to jump on the drawbar and ride like I did when I was a boy. An almost irresistible nostalgia swept over me. I even wished to have an F-20 in my garage parked next to my Ford sedan.

I asked myself why I'm so fascinated with old tractors. Part of it has to do with the passing of an era when a farmer made a comfortable living on a 200-acre farm with a dairy herd. Small farms dotted the Pennsylvania landscape where I grew up. We knew our neighbors and helped each other with threshing during harvesttime. We met at the feed store in the winter to repair old farm implements and to learn how to achieve higher crop yields.

Today the small farmer is an endangered species. The large corporate farmers plant and harvest thousands of acres with machines that cost as much as $100,000 or more. An era has passed yet my affections remain. F-20s are still my fond memory of boyhood, but I'd love to sit behind the steering wheel of a huge 10 wheeler with power steering and an air-conditioned cab, and cover more acres in an hour than our F-20 covered in a day.

It's difficult to move from one era to another, especially when the previous era matched your comfort level. As I visited Catholic families in New Haven, Connecticut after Vatican II, I heard people say, "I don't attend church anymore. St. Ann's isn't my church anymore now that the mass is in English. They've taken away the heart from the mass. No Latin? It's just not the same."

A friend of mine is 80. He laments about the newer praise songs in church. He says, "These songs are shallow. The same words over and over! There's no depth to them. Give me Isaac Watts!"

I smile to myself because my friend drives to church in one of the latest Lincoln town cars. He no longer chugs to church in a '39 Chevy.

There's a lot to be said for the olden days, but too often they are over-romanticized. Yes, people took time to be neighborly, but rapid transportation opened doors to broader communities and friends.

My wife and I flew to Mexico to participate in a family life conference. There we made many friends that we now chat with via e-mail.

Years ago my world was limited to a few friends in the township from which I seldom departed. Years ago I made church bulletins by typing an awkward stencil, placing it on a messy drum of a mimeograph machine, and cranking it by hand. It took half a day. Now I can insert fresh data into a computer template, click on the number of copies I need, and the job is done is less than an hour.

Oh, I used to grumble about praise songs, but I noticed that worship is more joyful and uplifting than when I was a boy. I see smiles instead of long faces. A triumphant feeling has replaced a somber mood.

Do I long for some elements of a bygone era? Of course I do, but if the new era can improve my friendship with Jesus, I'm going to do my utmost to benefit from the best of the new.

PASSING THIS WAY AGAIN

My neighbor farms the old-fashioned way. In the summer he runs his horse-drawn binder through his oat field and then stacks the sheaves into shocks. When the community threshing machine (or separator) came to his farm, I rode my bicycle over to watch the straw flying 50 feet from the thresher. I ran my hands through the oats pouring into the gravity-feed wagon.

When the huge Percherons pulled an empty wagon away from the machine, I jumped on the wagon and headed for the field with two farmers. For an hour I pitched sheaves to a farmer on the wagon, who stacked them in an interlocking fashion to keep the load from shifting.

When the wagon was full, I climbed to the top and rode back to the threshing machine. As I bounced atop the load, I realized that I had not done this for 55 years. It was like returning to my boyhood.

Returning to earlier days stirs the hearts of many adults. My son took his family back to his boyhood haunts in New England. They leapt off a bank on a rope swing and dropped into the frigid river at Jigger Johnson campground. They visited Thunder Hole and Cadillac Mountain in Acadia National Park. They swam in the icy water at Sand Beach.

In high school literature class I read that we pass this way but once. That may be true, but some of us try to pass this way again. I wonder if this is due to the fact that we were designed for eternity instead of three score and 10 years.

We will get the privilege of passing this way again. The Lord will make our blighted world new again and restore us to the intended eternal state. We'll plant and harvest and enjoy the fruits of our labors. The real bonus is that we will have the youthful spring in our step that will never fade into old age. At every turn of eternity new adventures will be ours.

The Bible doesn't tell much about the new earth, perhaps because we couldn't begin to grasp the grandeur of a life we have never dreamed of. Maybe God wants the new earth to overflow with surprises. Our fondest childhood memories will pale when we begin to work and play in eternal childhood.

The fantastic privilege of our eternal home is the ability to repeat the same thrills no matter how long time goes by—if time actually goes by. The saying that we pass this way but once will have no bearing on us then.

IT DOESN'T SEEM LARGE ANYMORE

I returned to Pennsylvania to preside at my brother's funeral. I deliberately arrived early so I could visit where I was born and grew up. The unnamed township road is now Culvert Road. The sandstone railroad underpass is much smaller and narrower than I remembered. It's still necessary to blow the car horn before entering the one lane, because the road immediately turns a sharp left on the other side. The rails are all torn up, because the Cornwall ore mine is closed. No trains carry iron ore to the smelter in Lebanon. The large Fairbanks scale house no longer stands along the tracks across from our barn—in fact, the barn that burned down when we lived there was never rebuilt.

The farmhouse looked so small I couldn't imagine my parents and eight children living in it. The corn shed still stands, but it has also shrunken in size. Why, my sisters and I used to roller skate on the smooth wooden floor of that shed. It seemed massive then.

I drove the half mile to the home where I lived until I was 4. The cement block garage that housed my father's Essex car is now too small for the modern car parked in front of it. My grandmother's house down the hill now looks considerably smaller than when I visited to sell garden seeds to Grandma.

I drove a mile north to see the neighbor's field where I picked tomatoes to earn money for school clothes. Back then I thought I'd never get to the end of the rows, but now that field is much smaller. Strange!

For years I boasted about the huge plantation house we lived in for a year in Peach Bottom. The Cornwall barn burned, and my family moved 50 miles south. I drove to the plantation house, and my wife and I were given a tour of the newly renovated home. As we walked through the rooms, I was struck with the smallness of the rooms. My wife said, "This doesn't seem as big as you described."

The Cherry Hill one-room school I attended has been converted to a residence, but it was far too small to hold 25 students. The yard where we played softball was not long enough for the home runs the big boys hit. How could everything change so much?

The world seen through the eyes of a child must seem larger than life. This is apparently true of physical features, but perhaps it is true of relational aspects of life as well. As I drove by the large elementary school in Cornwall, I thought about Valentines Day in the fifth grade. I gave Sylvia a special Valentine, but she sent my friend Harry two Valentines—big ones. I received a tiny one from her, and it did not have the word "love" before her name. I was crushed. I chuckle at the incident now, but it was no laughing matter in 1944.

I have experienced situations in adulthood that seemed enormously important at the time they occurred. I even lost sleep over some of them. Now that time has passed, and I have asked God to change my perspective on them, I no longer dwell on those times. In the light of eternity I wonder why they loomed so large.

Some of the hurts I've felt have been washed away to nothing because forgiveness has changed my perspective and my attitude. Offenses that seemed huge have been reduced to tiny bumps in the road.

I like to hold on to the big things in my childhood environment. I will not change their size, because that is part of my happy boyhood days. When it comes to the one-time big hurdles in adulthood, I'd just as soon shrink them to insignificance.

CHAPTER 6

Your Beautiful Children

RESPECT THE CHILDREN

Five of my neighbor children went fishing in a stream near their farm one afternoon. The 5-year-old sister boasted of catching five of the six fish they presented to their mother. The largest was a four-inch sunfish. She had no fancy rod and reel, just a throw line, but she had out-fished her 10-year-old brother, who proudly sported a new rod and reel.

A deep sea fisherman wouldn't consider her catch very important, but her mother gave her plenty of praise.

My older brothers took me fishing at night. We swatted mosquitoes and complained about fish that weren't hungry. Just as my brothers gathered their tackle to leave, I had a bite on my line. I pulled and retrieved a 14-inch pike from the dark water. I was proud of my catch, but my oldest brother said, "I'm not taking you fishing anymore. You bring us bad luck." I went home feeling crushed and unappreciated. Didn't I deserve a wee bit of praise?

That unappreciated pike taught me the importance of praising children. I had a chance to practice it in San Gabriel, California. For a week I told stories and played my musical instruments for 400 children from kindergarten to sixth grade. The children wanted to share their musical talents with me. A fifth-grade girl from Thailand played her "kim" flawlessly. A fifth-grade boy played a difficult classical piano sonata with ease. The junior band and the recorder ensemble made a happy sound. I clapped and praised every performer. You should have seen their faces.

When we came to the last day each classroom presented to me scrapbooks and thank-you cards. Now my face beamed as I thanked them for their creative gifts. I was blessed by their generosity and gratitude.

In my center desk drawer is a smooth white stone with a man's face painted on it. It was a Christmas gift from one of my sons. I thanked him and praised his creativity. I have used it for a paper weight, but mostly it occupies a place in my drawer as a reminder of his love. Some day when I'm gone, I hope he will find my treasured stone and feel my approval once more.

There are two people I'd like to meet and praise. One is a little boy who drew a picture for his father. It was the typical picture drawn by a 3-year-old. Stick arms and legs, head too large for the body, and hair that didn't touch the head. The whole picture demonstrated the normal undeveloped eye-hand coordination.

He was very pleased to give it to his father. He waited for words of appreciation, but his father said, "Do you know what you can do to *really* make your daddy happy? Draw me a really good picture."

I would like to tell that boy what a good job he did. I'd like to see the look of pride on his face that would result.

Another is now a grown man. I heard his horn solo when he was a teenager. I'd like to tell him how I enjoyed his horn concerto, one that I have heard professionals play with bloopers. So why fuss about one little mistake?

When the recital ended his perfectionist father picked apart his performance like a New York *Times* music critic. Not a word of commendation.

I know what it means to a kid to be complimented. I played third trumpet in the high school band when I was in grade school. I never had a solo part, just the um-pa-pa offbeat notes of a simple Sousa march.

The band performed at a summer festival in Jonestown, Pennsylvania. Between marches my father stood behind me and talked to a total stranger. "You wanna hear a boy who really knows how to play trumpet? Listen to this boy right here."

My father's words still puff up my chest when I feel down. I practiced harder than ever to become the trumpeter my proud father thought me to be.

Some day soon Jesus is going to say to His children, "Well done, good and faithful servants. Enter into my joyful kingdom." I hope all the children who are starved for commendation from adults will be there to hear His words of praise—WELL DONE.

PARENTAL PROTECTION

Yes indeed, a red-winged blackbird closed the entrance of a large city hospital. I can attest to it, because I frequented that hospital in Battle Creek, Michigan.

A pair of red-winged blackbirds decided to set up their maternity ward on a ledge by the main hospital entrance. Once the eggs were neatly tucked into the soft nest, both parents furiously guarded their territory. Visitors and hospital staff posed a threat simply by entering the hospital. The feisty birds dived on the unwary trespassers, and flopped their heads with their wings and pecked at their scalps. Ladies with puffy hairdos seemed to get the most punishment.

The hospital administrator ordered the front entrance closed and barricaded, and an alternate entrance established until the chicks were ready to leave the nest.

Never doubt the parental protectiveness of these sassy birds. You have probably seen them chasing crows and buzzards far from their nests. They always seem to win.

Gulls are just as vigilant about protecting their nests. A friend invited me to follow him to a gull nesting ground. Dozens of gulls had laid eggs on the ground without the protection of a soft nest. Everywhere we looked were gulls sitting on eggs.

Our two automobiles frightened the gulls. My friend rolled down his car window so he could hear them. In a few moments he opened the door and walked toward the nests. That was a mistake. Dozens of gulls swooped down, striking him on the head, while others dive-bombed his open car door and covered his seat with their excrement. Luckily, I had kept my windows closed and watched from the safety of my Ford.

Every spring a pair of killdeers nest in my front yard. For a month I avoid mowing a large area around their nest They have a curious way of protecting their nest. They run to another part of the yard and act like they are crippled. This draws attention away from their nest. Once the young hatch they run rapidly and do the fake-crippled act identical to their parents.

God placed a protective spirit in these creatures to defend their defenseless young. His crowning act of creation was the creation of the human family. It seems reasonable to expect them to defend their young, but some of my trips to the shopping mall or grocery store cause me to wonder.

The world watched in shock as a mother cruelly beat her child, the frightening act captured by a surveillance camera. Frequently the news tells of children chained to their beds or confined to closets and fed a starvation diet. These are extreme, but criminal acts. I hear parents in public places using cruel and toxic language with their children. They slap, shake, and yank them by the arms.

Dr. James J. Lynch shows in his research that children exposed to toxic words, bullying, and harassment carry the damage into adulthood, and become susceptible to chronic loneliness. They are often underachievers, which causes them to suffer from what he calls communicable disease.

In her 25-year study of children of divorce, Dr. Judith Wallerstein established that there are unexpected and lasting negative carryovers into adulthood. Selfish parents are so focused on their own issues that they fail to protect their young.

Isn't it strange that blackbirds, gulls, and killdeer take on creatures far larger than they to protect their young, yet humans abuse their young to vent their anger or practice their perversions on their own flesh and blood. Jesus said that "if anyone causes one of these little ones who believe in me to sin, it would be better for him to be thrown into the sea with a large millstone tied around his neck" (Mark 9:42, NIV). Sound harsh? Not when you consider the lasting effects of child abuse.

Some churches believe Sabbath School and Sunday School are for children, but the worship service is for adults. They forbid children to enter the worship experience. "Sing those little songs someplace," they say, "but please don't sing them in the worship service." Jesus said, "Forbid them not."

Every Sabbath in a small church I invited the children to be my choir. We sang the simple songs they loved. A little foster girl always requested "Jesus Loves Me." Every week she sang it with a broad smile on her face. One Sabbath she was missing. The court sent her back into a filthy and abusive home. She sent me a homemade card in which she wrote the words "Jesus loves me." In a few months people in authority worked in her behalf. She was returned to the foster home and back to our worship service. You guessed it. Her first song request was "Jesus Loves Me." The entire congregation sang it with her. We truly worshiped that Sabbath.

Protecting children physically, emotionally, and spiritually is a Christian responsibility. It is joining in the ministry of Jesus.

LIKE A LITTLE CHILD

Sitting in my doctor's waiting room I noticed a mother and a 2-year-old boy enter. The little tyke was jabbering words that only he understood. I looked up from my magazine, smiled at him, and made a funny face. That made him jabber all the more. In a few moments he slid off his mother's lap and ran to me with his arms outstretched. Instinctively I picked him up and sat him on my knee. His mother looked on approvingly.

As I sat in the men's department (two chairs for bored husbands while their wives shop) at Kohl's department store, I noticed an Indian family entering the store. A little girl about 3, with black hair and black eyes to match, spied a huge pile of stuffed toys. She touched them admiringly while her mother tried to coax her to follow her. Suddenly she turned and saw me. "Hi there!" she greeted. I returned her greeting, and she looked back at me with a smile as her mother dragged her to the ladies department.

I stopped by a neighbor's house to drop off some cough medicine. Four-year-old Robert took me by the hand and led me to the living room where he had dumped his building blocks on the floor. He could speak only German, but his message was clearly an invitation to help him build a house. I sat on the floor and was soon joined by his little brother We had a great time in the construction business.

I love the trust and playfulness of children. I have an idea that Jesus played blocks with children. Maybe that's how he came up with the idea that we must become like little children to enter the kingdom. (Now, don't try to prove that theologically.)

Why is it that some boys and girls grow up and forget how to trust and play?

My sons and I conducted one of the first father-son retreats in Michigan. The largest part of the program was fun and games in which fathers and sons had to interact. The first activity was constructing an object that depicted a memorable event in their father-son relationship We filled three tables with paper, glue, rubber bands, feathers, cotton balls, drinking straws, tooth picks, beads, and dozens of other items.

The sons promptly gathered their choice of items and returned to their fathers. They began building, but the fathers held back. It took a good 15 minutes for them to become engaged in the activity. One of my sons said, "Look, Daddy, these men have forgotten how to play."

Years ago I read a poem about how there will be no old people in heaven. The message was simple. God wants the trust and playfulness of a child to remain in us no matter our age.

My son expressed disappointment at having an "old lady" for a teacher in his new classroom. In a few days he reported that his teacher was a "neat" woman. She played softball with the students. She was short and stout and couldn't run bases very fast, but she could really slug the ball. Each day she selected a student to run the bases for her. All the kids wanted to be on her team. She had not forgotten how to play. For that reason the kids trusted her implicitly.

I sat by a swimming pool and watched a father supporting his little girl as she kicked and splashed with arms and legs. Another father stood at the deep end of the pool and caught his little boy when he came down the waterslide. He promised his boy to catch him and he did. Over and over the boy went down the slide. He knew his father wouldn't allow him to sink.

Jesus made it a practice to protect children. When his disciples scolded mothers for bringing children to Jesus, he quickly set them straight. He welcomed children into His presence. The church must do the same. The church cannot afford to force children to play with felts, color pictures, and make figures out of pipe cleaners during the hour of worship. The children know how to praise God. The church must make worship attractive to children.

A LITTLE BOY MECHANIC

Our little Daihatsu car groaned as it carried three of us and a translator to the little village of Manabao in the Dominican Republic. Our first stop was the village schoolteacher's home. The earthen floor was freshly swept with a palm broom. They had 13 children, a badge of honor in Manabao. They demonstrated their hospitality by serving the customary black coffee. They were thrilled that we wanted to take a picture of the whole family before we left.

Our final stop was a visit to the mayor's home. My friend backed the car against a dirt bank to keep it from rolling during our visit. We held the new baby and ate some of the root vegetables they were having for supper. It was getting dark, and we left as the father lit lamps made of peanut butter jars filled with oil and a wick placed through the jar lid.

When my friend turned the ignition key the motor ran a few seconds and sputtered to a stop. Again and again he tried, but to no avail. I pushed the little car so that he could start it by releasing the clutch while in gear, but that didn't work.

A young boy riding a little horse stopped. "Do you have motor problems?" he asked. "I can fix your motor," he boasted, as he lifted the hood. "Do you have sandpaper?" he asked. The translator gave him a fingernail file from her purse. He removed the distributor cap, filed the points, then replaced the cap. He closed the hood and ordered, "Start her up!"

Nothing but a sputter!

A teenager on a bicycle stopped "Are you having motor trouble?" he asked. "I can fix your motor," he boasted. "Do you have sandpaper?" he asked. The translator gave him the fingernail file that the first boy returned. He removed the distributor cap, filed the points, then replaced the cap. He closed the hood and ordered, "Start her up!"

Nothing but a sputter.

An old pickup truck rumbled down the dirt road, kicking up a cloud of dust. The driver stopped, jumped out, and said, "Do you have motor problems? I can fix your motor," he boasted. "Do you have sandpaper?" he asked. The translator gave him the fingernail file that the second boy returned. He lifted the hood, removed the distributor cap, filed the points, returned the cap, then slammed down the hood. "Start her up!" he ordered.

Nothing but a sputter.

"I'll tie my rope to your bumper and pull you to the center of the village," he offered "The best mechanic in the country lives here. He's a cab driver and knows all about cars."

There was no electricity in the entire village, but as the little Daihatsu was untied from the truck, the moonlight revealed a short man sauntering toward the car. He was the master mechanic. "Do you have motor trouble?" he asked. "I can fix any problem you have," he boasted. "Do you have sandpaper?" he asked. The translator gave him the fingernail file that the truck driver returned. He lifted the hood, removed the distributor cap, filed the points, replaced the cap, then slammed down the hood and ordered, "Start her up!"

Nothing but a sputter.

"You have a very defective car. You will have to stay here for the night and take this car to the factory dealer in the morning," he announced.

As he was delivering the bad news, I noticed a 6-year-old boy sitting on the ground behind the Daihatsu. He had a flashlight in one hand. With the other hand he was pushing a screwdriver up the exhaust pipe. When he had removed all the dirt that was packed into it when the driver backed the car into the bank, he stood up and ordered, "Start her up!"

The taxi driver slipped behind the steering wheel and turned the ignition key. Instantly the motor came to life. He closed the door and drove it rapidly around the village. He stopped the car next to us, climbed out, and said, "Your car is all fixed."

The driver pulled a $5 bill from his wallet while the translator told the taxi driver to be sure to give the boy part of the money.

I heard the matriarch of Manabao intoning "Santa Maria, Santa Maria." I hoped she was praying that the little boy really would get his share.

I returned to my lodging place in Jarabacoa convinced that children are important in God's scheme of things.

PORK BARREL AND KIDS

His red-striped shirt hung over his belt, his long arms and legs like pencils. He stood with his 20 fellow class members from the fifth-grade Bible class, singing a song to the adult church. His head was bent down so far that only his glasses and forehead were clearly visible. His lips barely moved as he faked the words of the song. All during the performance he never looked up. When the song ended he returned to his pew without raising his head.

That shy and skinny foster child haunted me for days. What was he thinking about? Did he feel worthless after being bounced from one foster home to another? Will he go through the rest of his life ashamed and with his head down?

He made me think about the wispy boy who spent a summer on my parents' farm. He was a "sunshine boy," a welfare lad from Philadelphia sponsored by an agency for poor families. His arms and legs were skinny just like the boy in church. His complexion was sallow, and his hair was dull and dirty. He was unresponsive to my mother's affection, almost like he didn't know what to do with it.

Roy also came to mind. He lived in a miners' village a mile from our farm. He was malnourished and spindly He came to spend many summer days with us, because his mother spent most of her days hanging out at the beer joints. Ray slept in the bathtub most nights because his bedroom was occupied by the men his mother brought to spend the night.

I think of the hundreds of children who sleep in shelters for the homeless every night in America. The land of plenty spends millions of dollars on defense, winning elections, lobbying politicians, feeding pets, and pork barrel projects attached to lame congressional bills, yet has not solved the problems of the poor and the elderly. Politicians allow billions to construct a space station, yet they cannot solve the problems of homelessness and child abuse.

A young child in Fort Worth, Texas, had her priorities straight. Her school visited the science museum and ate their sack lunches in a nearby park. She saw a bag lady searching all the trash cans for food. When the little girl returned home, she insisted on taking a bag of food back to the park for the bag lady. She found the lady and had the privilege of seeing her grateful smile. She was just a small child, but she knew how to put first things first.

CHAPTER 7

Putting Life in Church

LET'S HAVE A FROLIC

When one of my Amish neighbors needs to build a house or a barn they announce a frolic. It's what some folk call a work bee. Amish men and women come from miles around, ready to build or help with cooking. A good sized building can be constructed in a couple days.

I told my Amish neighbor that I'd be happy to join a frolic. By the time I arrived one day, more than a dozen men were already climbing on the frame of the house. At first I handed lumber to men on the second story. Finally I helped to nail down flooring.

A young man next to me bent a nail by accident. He pounded it into the wood, then circled it with his pencil and wrote the name of the man next to him by the circle. Laughter rang out to lighten the work. Water delivered by an 8-year-old boy quenched our thirst.

At noon we washed our hands and gathered around a long farm table. The women passed around many kinds of food followed by four kinds of dessert. At the end of the day we ate pumpkin squares and drank spearmint tea. Half of the men climbed into their buggies and headed home to milk their cows. The rest of us drank more tea and talked about milk prices and upcoming auctions.

The prophet Isaiah speaks about building houses and inhabiting them in the new earth, planting vineyards and eating the fruit. Jesus promised to make dwelling places for us in heaven, but the earth made new will be our time to design and build our own.

Do you suppose we'll have frolics in the new earth? I can imagine putting Noah in charge of framing my house. No problem with weather proofing! Maybe Joseph could supervise the trim carpentry. Perhaps Solomon would drop by to suggest how to dress up the front for curb appeal.

I can picture a long table set with the shiniest dinnerware, loaded with fruits and vegetables with the ideal degree of ripeness. No fruit tastes bitter because it was picked green and shipped from 2,000 miles away. We'd sit around the table and talk about the joy of living in our houses forever. I hope there will be frolics in the new earth.

Wait a minute! What about learning to do frolics in this present earth?

One of my parishioners in Connecticut was injured while his new house was half built. Members of the church finished it. I remember stapling insulation into the walls.

The community of faith could give the world an appetite for heaven if they had more frolics. Think of it as construction evangelism. A struggling family down the street from the church has a house that is too small for the family, but they can't afford an addition. An architect from the church visits the family and volunteers to sketch an addition to their liking. The church hires an excavator to dig the footers, and a week later a framing crew from the church descends upon the site. The addition is shelled in one day. A week later roofing and siding are installed, the interior is finished, and the family moves in at no cost.

Sound like an impractical pipe dream? I think not. Too expensive? Not at all. It would be the best public relations exercise done by the church in years. Putting a struggling family on their feet would demonstrate what Jesus said. "Inasmuch as ye have done it unto one of the least of these . . . ye have done it unto me" (Matt. 25:40, NKJV).

What do you say we have some frolics?

LIVING REMINDERS OF JESUS

My flight to Monterrey, Mexico, was five hours late. When I finished with customs I pulled my suitcases into a waiting crowd, but I didn't see anyone waiting for me. The airport information officer paged for anyone waiting for me to come to the information desk, but no one responded.

The airport officer told me I could make a collect call to the university where I was to speak, but I hesitated to do so. A man standing next to me said, "I have the solution to your problem. Give me the phone number. I'll call on my cell phone."

"But it is a long distance call," I protested.

"Of course it is," he replied. "My phone will reach that far." He flipped open his phone and dialed the number. The operator told me to call back in 15 minutes, and he would tell me who would be coming to pick me up. I hesitated again, because I was limited to a collect call. The man said, "Say yes. I'll be here with my cell phone."

Fifteen minutes later I received good news, thanks to his cell phone. When my ride arrived a few minutes later, I offered to pay him for his long distance calls. He said, "No, sir. I'm a Christian. Have you ever heard of the golden rule?" He rose from his seat and gave me a big embrace.

So many Christians have touched my life in a positive manner.

If I had no other validation for the existence of God, the providence from the hands of God's children would suffice.

My wife and I were to fly to British Columbia for a speaking engagement while strawberries were beginning to ripen in Michigan. We would not be able to resupply our stock of frozen strawberries for the winter.

An Amish family near our home learned of our situation. They had a large strawberry patch that ripened before we left. They told us to come over and pick them by 10:00 in the morning. By the time we arrived they had picked 16 gallons of berries for us and insisted on helping us hull them.

I asked them how much I owed. They promptly said, "Larry, I refuse to take anything. That's what neighbors are for." Mind you, this family had 10 children. I thought they surely could eat all the berries they grew, but they lived by the Christian ethic of sharing.

When we lived in New Haven, Connecticut, a short, bald German man brought us a loaf of genuine German rye fresh from a local bakery. This was his weekly ritual.

While living one summer in Portsmouth, Ohio, Christian neighbors and friends brought sweet corn, red beets, carrots, tomatoes, and squash to our doorstep. They did it quietly while we were still sleeping so as not to be identified.

I spent a summer selling books for a scholarship. Daisy Brittingham gave us the use of her cottage in Manchester, Ohio. While I was gone during the day, people would bring kettles of scrumptious food and place them on the table. Everyone knew that the house key was kept in a fuse box on the front porch wall. What a surprise to open the icebox and see a fresh strawberry pie or bowl of tapioca pudding! I had a standing invitation for Sunday breakfast at Fanny Coleman's home. She served corn on the cob—a new and mouth-watering delight for me. Southern biscuits and her husband's own honey left a sweet taste in my mouth for hours.

Selling near the little town of Rome, Ohio, I often ate lunch with the Colvins. They lived in a house with high ceilings and those long windows that reached from near the floor almost to the ceiling. The slightest breeze cooled the house on a warm day. We always ended lunch with a tall glass of lemonade on the veranda facing the Ohio River.

During the last third of the summer I took my meals with the Clarke family. Grandma Clarke and I picked apples from trees along the road, then she'd make stewed apples. We ate them with toast and whole milk. Her favorite dessert was banana pudding with vanilla wafers. I'd give about anything to have meals made by Grandma Clarke again.

Kindness? You bet! Oh, some say that Christians aren't the only ones who show it. I'd agree, but I also am convinced that it is God who motivates and enables them to be kind

Jesus spoke about God-followers traveling an extra mile to do a favor. In today's vernacular we say that Christians will give you the shirt off their back. That's what Christians do.

The problem comes when professed Christians act like the devil. It's what the decalogue calls taking the name of the Lord in vain.

In my travels I have felt the touch of Jesus through the generosity and sensitivity of His followers. I'm grateful for these living reminders of Jesus.

BOX SOCIAL

A pretty girl struck my fancy when I was 12. We talked frequently and entered into the sledding parties in wintertime. It was a thrill to have her join me on my Flexible Flyer.

Our church announced that there would be a box social. Women and girls were asked to bring a lunch in a box. The men and boys drew a number from a fishbowl. I drew the number of a box lunch made by an old lady and had to eat with her. The girl of my dreams ate lunch with a fellow she did not deserve.

By the end of the meal I had more than my share of multi-generational social life. Apparently the planners of the occasion didn't think how embarrassing a situation like mine could be. Maybe they had the same view held by some churches where a youth pastor friend of mine worked. They didn't understand why youth had to have something planned especially for them. My friend has been youth pastor of three churches and has yet to find a youth-friendly congregation.

Early youth ministers tried to entertain youth. They planned some great extravaganzas and the youth came, but when the youth pastor left, the kids began hanging out in the parking lot of the church instead of attending meetings.

It appears that youth are more interested in practical, necessary endeavors in which their involvement makes a difference. Volunteering among youth is on the rise. Interest in short term mission trips has been high.

A group of teenagers visited every home in a small New England town. They offered to clean house for the elderly, run errands, and arrange for transportation to doctor appointments. Some even invited lonely people for Thanksgiving dinner. People were stunned by the depth and sincerity of their visitors. As the youth cleaned an elderly man's house, he sat in his recliner and repeated over and over, "I can't believe this is happening."

My denomination came up with a slogan—Give the youth a piece of the pie. I maintain that we should invite them for the whole meal. We have yet to successfully integrate youth into the life of the church, particularly the worship services.

Can youth really speak to the needs of parishioners in worship? Oh yes. When I was sophomore in high school I was part of a ministry group. I preached the sermon in a small northern Pennsylvania church. Decades later I visited that church. An elderly woman grasped me by the arm and told me how much my sermon had helped her over the years. She still remembered my illustrations.

Miraculous things happen when we invite children and youth to stay for the whole meal.

RECLUSES

Every time our family visited Grandma Alleman in Hummelstown, Pennsylvania, my father drove past a crudely made gate stretched across a narrow foot path. Cowbells and tin cans hung along the barbed wire, along with signs—KEEP OUT, MAD DOG, POSTED, STAY AWAY. I never saw signs of life, not even a house.

My father told me that a hermit lived in a cave far back on the trail. Few people knew him by name. He ventured out for groceries when he would be least noticed. I told my father I'd like to meet him, but my father said he would probably not appreciate my overtures of friendship.

Many years later I visited Jerome, Arizona, where I paid a few dollars to enter a ghost town. On the edge of the town I noticed a sign that read VISIT THE CAVE MAN, with an arrow pointing up a steep mountain trail. Now was my chance to meet a recluse.

In the distance I saw what looked like half of a log cabin across the trail. The door was open. I heard a voice inviting me to enter. Sitting on an old army cot covered with a woolen army blanket was a 48-year-old man. He gave us a tour of his half-cave, half-cabin home. The owner of the ghost town built the cabin after the recluse had lived in the cave for a year. He had running water piped from a spring on the mountain. He cooked his food on a potbellied stove vented to the outside with a long stovepipe.

He was unable to tolerate large groups of people, so he asked permission to live in the cave. Each week he walked to Cottonwood and received free food from churches. He spent time reading and keeping a scrapbook of photos taken with guests to his cave. After my visit I sent him a book about a man who lived in a cave before giving his life to Christ. My church friends sent him a new quilt to place on his cot. I hoped to receive a letter from him, but he never wrote.

Is being a recluse God's design for life? Do we not exist for a greater purpose than living within a narrow comfort zone?

The New Testament says that Jesus grew in wisdom and stature, and in favor with God and people. Jesus was a people person. He loved to talk to and bless children. He went to weddings and feasts provided by people of wealth. He mingled with people of all walks of life. When He died, rose again, and ascended to heaven, there was a noticeable void on the village streets.

Jesus said that we are the salt of the earth and the light of the world. Salt is worthless if kept in the shaker. Light has no value if hidden in a cave. We need to mingle with others for their benefit and ours.

Jesus demonstrated this ideal. He went into the presence of the Father to be filled with compassion and grace, then He went into the presence of people to bless them and be blessed by them.

We can be a source of encouragement to others if we have a regular time of recuperation with God. If filled by God, we can spill joy into others.

YOU NEED A FRIEND

Leaders of a large Bible church asked me to meet with a group of grieving people. They estimated the attendance would be two dozen. To their surprise their large church was nearly full.

A friend had quietly told me that a young man afflicted with Lou Gehrig's disease, and his wife of less than a year, would be attending.

After a few opening remarks, I asked people to share their sorrow. I roamed around the church with a microphone and allowed them to minister to each other.

I noticed a young man strapped to a high-backed wheelchair. His beautiful brunette wife sat close to him. I was sure this was the newlywed couple.

Joan slowly rose to her feet, struggling to keep her composure. "Please," she asked, "tell me what we can do with the pain. What do we do with the pain?"

I turned to the large audience and said, "Some of you must also know pain. Do you have an answer for this couple?"

A middle-aged woman raised her hand. She took the microphone and said, "I want to look into your faces and speak from my heart. My husband recently died after a long battle with ALS. We had emotional pain that would not go away. We had to experience the pain. The only way we survived was with the blessing of friends who were not afraid to stay by our side. Friends made the difference. What you need is a friend. *I will be your friend.*"

On the opposite side of the church another woman stood and said, "I went through this with my husband. If it had not been for friends, I don't know what would have become of me. *I'll be your friend.*"

Person after person rose and promised to be their friends. After many offers I said, "As soon as this meeting ends, all of you friends need to exchange phone numbers and addresses." When the meeting ended the beautiful couple were surrounded. They received the best antidote for pain—friendship.

When pain stabs at the human heart, words are usually inadequate. A friend who is willing to sit by the side of a wounded soul, to sit in silence not knowing what to say, but knowing she wants to be there, is a soother of the sorrowing. Henri J. M. Nouwen expressed this sentiment and called such persons *living reminders of Jesus.*

Philip Yancey writes about the difficulty in believing in an invisible God. I have friends who received support during their bitter sadness. They speak of God's touch through the touch of faithful friends.

Jesus understood pain and suffering. He knew the value of supportive friends. As he entered the Garden of Gethsemane, he invited three of his disciples to join him in prayer. They slept, leaving Jesus to struggle alone. If Jesus knew the value of friendships during hard times, it is certainly appropriate for us to seek the support of friends.

During a clergy-family retreat a woman who had been traumatized by sexual abuse shared her pain. She courageously reached out for support.

An evangelist loudly declared, "Sister, all you need is Jesus!" Anger flared up within me, and I shot back, "Sir, you don't understand that there are times when Jesus is not enough!"

God arranged for the expansion of the human family precisely because he wanted us to have friends to support us

I read a book written by a Dinka boy from Sudan who was forced into slavery for 10 years. His only human contact was a master who forced him to work under the threat of having his hands cut off if he tried to escape. His sorrow and pain mounted daily, because he didn't have anyone to call his friend.

The real challenge of the church is to make sure that none of the members can say, "I don't have a friend." The church has a mandate to heal the wounds of those within the church so that the same mandate can be met beyond the walls of the church.

My audience had it right when they told the newlyweds, "What you need is a friend. We'll be your friend."

CHAPTER 8

Living With a Difference

BREAKING DOWN WALLS

During chaplaincy training I was required to choose a partner with whom I could share biographies. I chose William, a young Catholic priest about five years my junior. Each of us spent three hours of in-depth interviewing in order to write a comprehensive biography.

After the interviews ended, William said, "You are the first Protestant I have come to know. As a boy I was sent to a Catholic school, and my entire training was done exclusively in Catholic circles. It is so refreshing to know that Christians exist in other communions."

"That's interesting," I responded, "because before this exercise I had never known a Catholic at such a deep level. I grew up in a communion that had many negative comments to make about Catholics. I attended elementary school next to a large Catholic church. The parsonage stood next to the church. One day I saw the priest taking long drags on a large cigar. Slowly he blew the smoke on the roses blooming in the yard. I boldly asked him what he was doing. He smiled and said that he was blowing holy smoke on the roses to drive away the bugs. His humor made me think that Catholics must not be as bad as I was led to believe. Now that I've come to know you, I am also happy to know that God has His children in many communions."

William and I spent 12 weeks in close fellowship during our training program.

In that same program was a young Lutheran minister who held negative feelings toward me that never changed in 12 weeks. During one session we were required to state how we felt about each of the students.

The Lutheran minister looked at me with contempt and said, "I hate Larry. When I saw that a Seventh-day Adventist would be in this class I said, 'Oh God, not one of those.'"

The supervisor pushed him to be specific about why he hated me, but all he could do was reiterate his dislike for me. In spite of many attempts on my part, I could not change his feelings. His dislike of my religion kept him from getting to know me as a person. He had built a wall that kept us from knowing each other.

During my childhood I grew up in Amish and Mennonite territory in Pennsylvania. I saw their black buggies and automobiles with chrome painted black, but they were a mere curiosity to me. A veil of mystery hung between us. I heard people joking about them, but I seldom saw the admirable qualities of these faithful followers of Jesus.

Now I live in the center of 55 Amish families. I attend weddings, baptisms, and school programs, and worship with them from time to time. I play games with them, eat meals in their homes, and occasionally help them with farmwork. They are genuine Christian friends. The prejudice I learned as a boy has vanished.

How narrow our world is when we are ruled by ignorance. Walls block our view and rob us of rewarding relationships

For years I co-lectured in professional growth seminars for clergy of all faiths. New worlds opened as we shared ideas and ate together. We formed lasting friendships.

A Church of Christ pastor has been my friend for years. We share book ideas, have friendly conversations about our respective church doctrines and polity, and pray for each other when we face personal and family problems. I often think about how much enjoyment I would have missed by not opening my heart to his friendship.

Jesus spent a lot of energy breaking down walls as his disciples watched in amazement. He treated people as equals and potential citizens of the kingdom of heaven. The earliest Christian church was slow in learning this lesson. The church still struggles with wall building.

The owner of a new house built a stone wall across the front of his property. Every spring part of the wall collapses. He carefully rebuilds it. I noticed something curious about his wall. It is constructed out of round stones. There isn't a flat stone anywhere in the wall.

Walls in churches and in the secular world are like that Michigan wall. They are often made up of people who think alike and sometimes look alike. They are built to keep out anyone who is different.

I was the pastor of a large city church. Pride in the ethnic background of the church was strong. As the demographics of the city changed, people of other ethnic backgrounds began attending. People accused me of selling out the church to these groups. I was tearing down their walls built with round stones.

God loves to tear down walls. The once-impetuous Peter was sunning himself on a rooftop when God gave him a vision of many unclean animals in a sheet. God told him to eat, but Peter objected on the basis of their being unclean. God told him not to call them unclean. Of course, God was talking about non-Jews who were considered outside the realm of redemption. God tore down the wall of Peter's prejudice and opened the way for the rapid development of the community of faith.

I've learned that God can tear down walls in my mind. He can make my world bigger, friendlier, and more hospitable.

WE'RE ALL LOSERS

I attended a retreat for physicians and dentists in Canada, in an area where lumbering was the main industry. The first evening the professionals mingled with laughter and lively conversation.

My attention was drawn to a young man seated alone in one corner of the room. One of his hands had been amputated. It appeared that he was there to do the menial work such an occasion required. I watched him for more than an hour. None of the accomplished guests spoke to him.

I went over and introduced myself. He had worked in a large sawmill until the big saw took off one hand. Having little education, he was limited in finding work. The government promised to rehabilitate him and train him for some type of work. In the meantime he felt useless and worthless. In the company of "important people" he felt even more insignificant.

He sat with me at each meal. We talked about his interests and dreams. I let him know that the loss of a hand was not the loss of his mind. As we visited over three days, I watched a brightness creep across his countenance.

Society has a way of pegging people by what they do. Educational degrees, important as they are, have been the criteria of importance in some circles. When people meet, they seldom ask *who* you are. Usually they ask what you *do.*

One of my favorite airport activities during layovers is talking to custodial personnel who pick up unwanted newspapers and empty trash bins. I like to tell them that I appreciate the cleanliness of their airport.

At church I seek out the janitors and compliment them on keeping the premises spic and span. I tell them that they are just as vital to the church operation as the senior pastor. In the process I come to know who they are inside, not simply what they do.

One of my favorite authors, Robert Farrar Capon, says that Jesus will present all of us to the Father in the power of His resurrection, not by virtue of our records, good or bad. He states that God saves losers and only losers. He raises the dead and only the dead. He rejoices more over the lost, the last, the least, and the little than over the winners of the world.

In his book *The Parables of Grace,* Capon writes, "Jesus rubbed the salt of lostness on the sensibilities of those who are preoccupied with the sweetness of their own success." (Wm. B. Eerdmans Publishing, Grand Rapids: 1988, p. 36.)

Jesus took time to meet the needs of blind beggars. He restored a dead son to a widow. The sick man by the pool of Siloam left healed after decades of hopelessness. Jesus took interest in Zacchaeus—the despised tax gatherer. By no means did he disregard those in influential places. High or low, rich or poor, all were the same to him—children of the heavenly Father.

I was 16 when I left the farm and headed for Philadelphia to attend school. Sitting on the front porch of my boarding house on a sunny day, I watched as a street sweeper pushed his big broom down the gutters and placed the refuse in his large, wheeled trash can. Several ragmen pushed their carts past the house yelling "Rags!" One old man collected cardboard. His cart was stacked so high that he could scarcely see where he was going.

It dawned on me that these men were making Philadelphia livable. The "successful" people rushed to work in corporate offices, leaving the sanitation workers unnoticed, but without sweepers and collectors the city would have been awash in trash.

Some operate by the upward mobility philosophy in the church world. They leave pastoral ministry and happily assume administrative roles. Seldom do they return to pastoral ministry, seeing it as downward mobility. They remain in administration long after they are out of touch with what pastors face.

A Methodist minister told me that his denomination likes to move administrators back to pastoral positions to keep them practical. He reminded me that downward mobility was the philosophy of Jesus. He left glory to take on humanity. Thanks to His downward mobility, we now receive eternal life.

True upward mobility will come when the lost, the least, the last, and the little are redeemed completely upon Jesus' return. The Bible says we will meet him in the air. That's upward mobility!

BELOW THE SURFACE

A little girl asked her kindergarten teacher, "Are you Chinese?" Her teacher replied, "No, I'm a Korean." The little girl's classmates twittered, "What did she say?" The girl replied, "She said she's a crayon!"

Hearing and reading people inaccurately is also an adult trait.

I met a young man who wore his hair in a less conservative style than mine. His full beard and mustache made me strongly doubt his credibility. Within an hour I was awed by his intelligence and uncanny skills.

When I admired the cuckoo clock on his wall, he chuckled and told me, "That's a cheap clock made especially for gullible tourists in Europe. It's a piece of junk. My friend asked me to fix it for him." Then he described the problem in technical terms incomprehensible to me. Before I left I enjoyed the music and bird song on the hour.

From the backroom he brought an antique clock. All the inner workings were made of wood. Some gears were broken or missing. He showed me the gears he had made by hand. The tiny cogs on the gears were painstakingly made with a jeweler's saw and tiny files. The gears meshed with each other perfectly. He said it took 3 hours to make one gear, but he was making a jig that would reduce the time to one hour.

What skill! A clock museum and private clock owners for miles around sought his services.

My phone rang late one afternoon in the 1960s. A young woman told me she and her friend had hitchhiked from Boston to do gravestone rubbings. They had planned to spend the night with a friend, but the friend was not home. Did I know of any place where they could spend the night? I invited them to spend the night at our house, sight unseen.

When they climbed into my car at the Hudson, Massachusetts, town square, I was flabbergasted. The two hippie types had the natural look. They carried knapsacks in which they kept their rubbing tools.

My wife was taken aback when they walked through the front door, but her mother-heart sensed that they had not eaten in many hours. Soon we were seated around the table enjoying a delicious meal.

They told us about spending every summer volunteering at a New Hampshire camp for blind and handicapped children. They shared their joy in the Lord with us.

My wife opened the hide-a-bed and proceeded to bring sheets and blankets from the linen closet, but they insisted on sleeping in their clothes without bedding. They didn't want to create any extra laundry. In the morning we served a big breakfast. I took them to town where they stuck out their thumbs to catch a ride back to Boston.

A month later we received in the mail a gravestone rubbing of Mother Goose's tombstone located in a moss-covered cemetery in Boston. It was their thank-you gesture. Needless to say, the whole experience shattered our preconceived ideas about hippies.

Why do I sometimes expect the worst in people? Why do I read them inaccurately? How many more pleasant encounters will it take to teach me to look for the good in others?

Living With a Difference

OLIVER

Oliver and I became best friends in the first grade. Neither of us were expert marble players. The boys all played for keeps, so Oliver and I went through bag after bag of marbles. We soon agreed that we could play just for fun, not for keeps, just the two of us. It was a great idea. We even played Jacks together. Mostly girls played Jacks, but that didn't matter to us.

One day I told Oliver that I could play the harmonica. I practiced until I could play "Polly Wolly Doodle" and "Oh, Susanna." Oliver told me he knew how to tap dance. At recess we did a little song and dance routine. Our teacher found out how talented we were. She included us in school programs.

Early in our friendship the older boys noticed our friendship. They began to threaten us by taking our coats and throwing them down the steep bank by the ball field. Eventually they grabbed us and threw us down the bank. They called us names that didn't make sense to me, but it was obvious to us that they were not nice names.

I told my older brother about our problem. He told me that the boys did not like Oliver because he was the only boy in school who had skin that was not white. Funny, I didn't notice that. He was just Oliver, my friend.

My father said he was not surprised at their behavior. He worked in the Cornwall ore mines with Oliver's father, and knew how the miners treated him.

My brother took matters in his own hands. The next morning he walked the one mile to school with me. We stopped in to see the justice of the peace along the way. My brother told him about the bullies. The justice asked me the names of the boys, then told me to go to school without fear.

That morning the justice of the peace called the bullies out of their classroom. With a stern voice he said, "I understand you boys are being rough on Oliver and Lawrence. If this happens one more time, I'm coming to take you to the mines. I know your fathers. I'll order your fathers to give you a good whipping. I mean every word of it, boys, so you'd better not rough up those boys one more time."

That ended the trouble. Oliver and I continued to be best friends until I moved away in the seventh grade.

Looking back I can understand the bullies' prejudice. The multi-ethnic communities that sprang up around the ore mines simmered with racial hatred. The various groups talked about each other, with demeaning names, but rarely with each other. The schoolyard bullies learned their attitudes from adults.

Oliver has never left my mind. At times I've been an Oliver. I took a position as chaplain in a Texas hospital. My speech betrayed me as "not from around here." Hearing my northern accent, a patient in the intensive care unit promptly told me to go back where I came from. His prejudice was alive and well in spite of his grave illness.

At my first ministerial association meeting in Texas, the association president embarrassed me in front of all the ministers in attendance. He ridiculed my denomination and my diet. I determined to meet him at his own game—with a different twist. I invited the association to hold their monthly meetings in my hospital, at no cost, with free lunch besides. I told them that they would receive a free guest card, which would get them a free meal anytime they visited parishioners in the hospital.

I marveled at how my antagonist's attitude changed when he learned more about me and my faith.

I often think about how much fun those bullies missed because they never took the time to know Oliver. They chose to be relationally poverty-stricken.

The early Christian Church was limping along until Peter had a vision of unclean animals in a sheet. God told him not to call any person unclean. The news spread and before long people of all backgrounds were rejoicing in the good news of salvation. I look forward to the day when the church will be one big happy family.

CHAPTER 9

The Blessed Hope

WILD-GOOSE CHASE

Recently moved to Texas, our family was eager to see the state where they sing *Don't Fence Me In*. Our newly acquired copy of *Texas Highways* magazine portrayed a historic village at Buffalo Gap. We climbed into the car and made our way from Fort Worth across the barren flatlands, where telephone poles look like skyscrapers. It was a long and boring drive, but we didn't mind. We knew we were in for a real treat.

In Buffalo Gap we saw no signs pointing us to the tourist attraction, so I asked directions from a gas-station attendant. I parked in front of a rundown building and entered the front door. A handmade sign indicated that admission was $4 per person. I reluctantly paid, and that began our tour of three or four buildings full of assorted junk. None of the items were labeled, nor were they tied to the history of Buffalo Gap. The only building of interest was the one owned by a village dentist. An odd array of rusting devices lay scattered on the ground outdoors.

In less than an hour we were headed home. A voice from the back seat piped up, "Boy, that was another one of Daddy's wild-goose chases."

That wasn't our last wild-goose chase in Texas. We decided to cool off from the Texan summer with a lake swim at Cleburne State Park. The water was as warm as bath water and swirled a muddy chocolate with every step.

Moving to Michigan, I had another wild-goose chase when I looked at a house for sale. The ad described a pleasant villa. The realtor began his positive sales pitch as we stepped onto the front porch. But as he gripped the front doorknob, the knob fell out in his hand. Everything went downhill from there.

A wild-goose chase is when our expectations and reality are miles apart. We look forward to something exciting, only to be let down.

My junior Sabbath school teacher told my class about heaven. She showed us pictures of heaven painted by a hopeful artist. Heaven was always bright, golden, and full of perfect flowers and fruit. Mrs. Brown's voice would choke up as she'd say, "Our eyes have not seen, nor our ears heard, the beautiful things God is preparing for us." She assured us that heaven is no wild-goose chase.

When God gave Moses the blueprint for making the tabernacle, He specified costly materials. The dwelling place of God must receive the greatest attention to detail. After all, it was a symbol of the heavenly dwelling place. Visiting the tabernacle reminded worshipers that heaven is not a wild-goose chase.

I had seen pictures of the Grand Canyon in *National Geographic* magazine, but when I walked to the edge of the rim and looked down and out, I was almost speechless. Its beauty surpassed all the photographs I had drooled over. I am still awestruck by the images of the canyon that I carry in my mind. Grand Canyon was no Buffalo Gap. It was no wild-goose chase.

When I walk through the gates of the heavenly city with my family and friends, I'm sure I will not hear anyone saying, "Is this it? What a letdown!"

If you are weary on your journey to the Kingdom of God, keep walking. You are not headed to Buffalo Gap.

DREAMS

Eighty-year-old Clara said to me, "Pastor, you must tell me the meaning of a dream I had this week. I found myself in a large room without windows. Suddenly hundreds of black ravens filled the room. They flew at me with their beaks ready to bite me. I picked up a board and began swinging at them, but I couldn't hit them. I got so tired that I fell to the floor. The ravens were all diving at me at once. Then I awakened. Now, what does this mean?"

I felt like the wise men in Nebuchadnezzar's court who couldn't reveal the king's dream, let alone tell the meaning. Clara was disappointed in me, but what could I do? I didn't know the meaning of my own dreams.

As a grade-schooler I often dreamed that I rode my scooter to school. On the way home a wicked witch chased me, but I managed to stay ahead of her. When I reached the farm, I climbed the ladder to the second floor of the cornshed. I went through the door to the upstairs and quickly locked it. I always woke before I could safely reach our warm kitchen.

The Babylonian wise men ended up before Nebuchadnezzar's executioners. Imagine how Daniel felt going before the ruthless ruler to tell him the dream and the interpretation. Yes, God gave him both, but old Neb was unpredictable. How could Daniel know his reactions?

As Daniel told the dream, Nebuchadnezzar's face must have brightened. "Ah, yes, that's it! How did you know?" he could have shouted.

Then the bad news followed. "You are the golden head and another empire will replace you," Daniel informed.

The smile left his face and defiance took its place. He would not have any golden head rolling in Babylon, so he built an image of solid gold.

Old Babylon fell despite the solid-gold image. Nothing could stand in the way of God's purposes. Kings and mighty potentates are no match for the Sovereign of the universe.

The Scripture declares that the King of kings will return to earth and send all the dictators, political manipulators, and selfish rulers scrambling to the rocky places to hide from His face, but there will be no place to hide.

Angry rulers in command of vast armies will flee from the face of Christ, their forces disbanded. Those who practiced ethnic cleansing will tremble before the Lord and His heavenly hosts. Their dreams of lasting power will vanish before the Lord of hosts. Kings and kingdoms will all pass away, and the Creator's Kingdom will be everlasting.

I have never dreamed about the climax of evil, but I have pondered what it will be like to see Jesus coming in the clouds of heaven. After Sabbath dinner I used to lie down on the lawn, look at the puffy clouds floating in the blue sky, and imagine His appearing.

If I ever have a dream about the second coming of Jesus, I won't have to hire a dream therapist. I'll know exactly the meaning. I'll believe it is real, because He has promised to come again. I may have to wait, but it will come true. God has a timetable. He keeps His appointments.

I'LL WAKE YOU ON TIME

Our wealthy landlord invited my parents, me, and three of my sisters to have dinner at his house in Bethesda, Maryland. This was a mighty treat for kids who seldom left the township in which they were born. To get there we took the train from Lebanon, Pennsylvania, to the central station in Washington D.C. My nose touched the window most of the way, looking at the new sights on my first train ride.

The chauffeur met us at the station. Our landlord's house was larger than any I had ever visited. A white starched tablecloth adorned the large dining-room table. I puzzled about which of the various forks and knives by my plate I should use. No big bowls of food decorated the table like at home. Instead, a black-suited butler, a white towel over his arm, brought each of us our food. By the time we finished the meal, I was a nervous wreck.

The chauffeur drove us back to the train station—back to a table with an oiled cloth cover, one of each utensil, and big bowls of food in the center that at times required the boarding house reach.

I distinctly recall my concern the night before we left for Bethesda. I worried that I would oversleep and miss my first train ride. When I expressed my apprehension to my mother, she said, "Don't you worry. I'll wake you up on time." I closed my eyes and slept soundly until my mother shook me awake. "It's time to get up," she called.

Now, I always tell adults not to tell children that their dead loved one is asleep. It could cause a child to be afraid to fall asleep. Yet when I read the Gospels, I notice that Jesus repeatedly called death sleep. Sleep implies that the sleeper will awaken. The word promises that death is not permanent.

When Jesus died on the cross, He died the second death for all who choose to follow Him. His followers don't need to fear the death from which there is no awakening. Their death is merely a sleep. Jesus assured His followers, "Don't worry. I'll wake you up on time."

The waking up time is the second coming of Jesus. It will be a surprise for the saints who are sleeping, even though they had that assurance before death. In Eugene H. Peterson's paraphrase of 1 Corinthians 15, he says, "You hear a blast to end all blasts from a trumpet, and in the time that you look up and blink your eyes—it's over. On signal from that trumpet from heaven, the dead will be up and out of their graves, beyond the reach of death, never to die again" (Message).

Peterson's rendition of 1 Thessalonians 4:16, 17 is even more exciting. "The Master himself will give the command. Archangel thunder! God's trumpet blast! He'll come down from heaven and the dead in Christ will rise—they'll go first Then the rest of us who are still alive at the time will be caught up with them into the clouds to meet the Master. Oh, we'll be walking on air! And then there will be one huge family reunion with the Master. So reassure one another with these words" (Message).

I like to use my imagination. If I die before Jesus comes back, I will be sleeping in the grave, unaware of anything going on in the world. The trumpet blast will signal a huge angel to come to my grave. With divine creative power I will emerge and come face to face with my angel "It's time to wake up," the angel will say. "I'm taking you to meet Jesus and all your family. We are going to heaven for dinner. You won't believe the menu and all of us angels will sing the dinner music. Hurry! Let's be on our way."

I don't know about you, but I'm ready for the trip. I'm going to have a view of space that will make the Hubble space telescope look like a child's toy. I'm not worrying about when it will happen, because Jesus has the time table fixed from eternity. He'll wake me up on time.